The EASTERN BEFORE BEECHING

The EASTERN BEFORE BEECHING

JOHN BRODRIBB

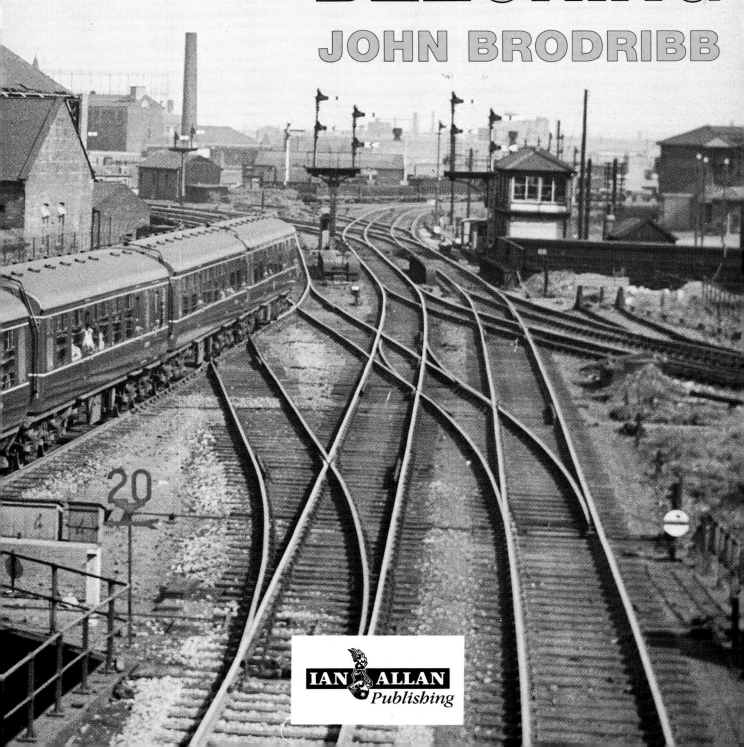

IAN ALLAN Publishing

First published 1994

ISBN 0 7110 2240 2

Designed by Ian Allan Studio

Published by Ian Allan Publishing: an imprint of Ian Allan Ltd, Terminal House, Station Approach, Shepperton, Surrey TW17 8AS; and printed by Ian Allan Printing Ltd Coombelands House, Coombelands Lane, Addlestone, Weybridge, Surrey KT15 1HY.

Previous page:
Leeds City-Harrogate diesel at Whitehall Junction, Leeds.
Eric Treacy

Front cover:
The colour illustration depicts Class Q6 63455 dividing its coal train at South Pelaw prior to tackling the Consett line on 20 September 1965.
Hugh Ballantyne
The other photographs on the cover are taken from inside the book.

Contents

Acknowledgments

I must acknowledge the help that a great number of people have given freely, and for which I am most grateful; the order in which they appear here has no significance. First of all to the staff at the Public Record Office, Kew; it is a pleasure to work there. I hope that the following list of individuals does not leave anyone out, and I apologise if it does: John Baker, Stan Hinbest, Gordon Wells, Peter Punchard, the late George Ewles, and all the photographers upon whose work I have drawn. I must also mention the Greenwood family, whose help makes research at the PRO much easier, and my wife Wendy for her unceasing encouragement and support.

It is also important to record that some of the best historical research is being done by the various specialist societies and associations, and in this context I can recommend contacting the following if more information is required:

M&GN Circle: G. L. Kenworthy, 16 Beverley Road, Brundall, Norwich NR13 5QS

North Eastern Railway Association: T. Morrell, 8 Prunus Avenue, Kingston Road, Willerby, Hull HU10 6PH

Great Eastern Railway Society: J. Tant, 9 Clare Road, Leytonstone, London E11 1JU

Great Central Railway Society: E. Latusek, 41 Spire Hollin, Glossop SW3 9BJ

Great Northern Railway Society: R. Tarpey, 16 White Leather Square, Billingborough, Lincs NG34 0QP

LNER Study Group: P. N. Hall, 57 North Road, Glossop SK13 9AU

The list was correct at the time of writing, and if anyone would like further information (I don't guarantee to have it!) they are welcome to contact me via Ian Allan Ltd. Please don't forget to enclose an SAE if you write to any of the groups noted above.

Finally, if there are any mistakes or obvious blunders, then I apologise – they are all mine; I'd be pleased to hear from anyone with comments, suggestions or additional information. Do get out and see some of the traditional railway while it remains – there is still much there, but it is vanishing rapidly. Alternatively, you can always get involved with one of the preservation schemes and help to recreate a little of it.

Introduction

The former London & North Eastern Railway had covered a substantial part of the eastern side of England, together with much of Scotland, its constituents having included a number of major English companies at the 1923 grouping: principally the Great Eastern, Great Northern, Great Central and North Eastern. This gave it two trunk routes to the north, from King's Cross and Marylebone, as well as the lines into East Anglia from Liverpool Street; the Great Eastern had even claimed to offer the 'Cathedrals Route' from London to York via Cambridge, Ely and Lincoln – although it hardly competed on speed with the Great Northern. It had a virtual monopoly in East Anglia (total after the takeover of the Midland & Great Northern Joint in 1936), as well as most of Lincolnshire and through into Yorkshire, Durham and Northumberland, where the North British – another LNER constituent – was also represented.

The initial organisation of British Railways saw the creation of Eastern and North Eastern Regions, broadly reflecting the former areas of the LNER, whilst the lines north of the border became part of the Scottish Region, together with those from the LMS. The Eastern and North Eastern Regions were amalgamated in 1968, and although that event is after the period related in this book, it is the territory of that larger Eastern Region that is covered in this book, even though it takes the story only as far as Dr Beeching's day.

There were, of course, a few other very minor lines that had not been part of one of the big companies, but which came into the LNER fold at the grouping. They included the Colne Valley from Chappel to Haverhill in Essex, the Mid-Suffolk Light and the Easingwold. The Eastern and North Eastern were thus sprawling conglomerations of immense contrasts, from the industrial heartlands of Tyneside to the agricultural centres of Lincolnshire. Much of the system was largely untouched by progress, for although the publicists had had a field day with the introduction of the streamliners on the ECML, the LNER had been too strapped for cash to do much about its rural retreats. The policy for up-and-coming staff was to start at the bottom, so aspiring stationmasters started with Class 4 jobs out in the country, where there was probably no running water, electricity, gas or any other modern convenience. Water would have to be pumped up, or drawn from a well, and a hip-bath used when the need arose. The station might well still be oil-lit (if indeed there were trains after dark – at least one on the North Eastern had converted its lamp holders to house hanging baskets!). The stationmaster would be a very important member of the local community, and some found the rural life so congenial that they never moved on. The LNER had regarded the branches as feeders to the rest of the system and kept them open wherever possible, though a few twigs (they were hardly even branches) had succumbed in the early 1930s, and even then usually lost only their passenger services, surviving for goods traffic into the 1960s and Dr Beeching's regime.

In 1948 nationalisation saw the Railway Executive take over from Britain's 'Big Four' companies, thus placing the railways under a single management for the first time. It had been threatened on a number of occasions for the best part of a century, and

Left:

A fine study of Abbotts Ripton station, between Huntingdon and Peterborough, with an up express approaching, headed by one of the new diesels. This view dates from July 1959, but the station has been closed to passengers for about nine months, as can be seen from the platform coping stones and corbels stacked by the buildings. Even so, it is otherwise intact – just look at that lamp!
Douglas Thompson

5

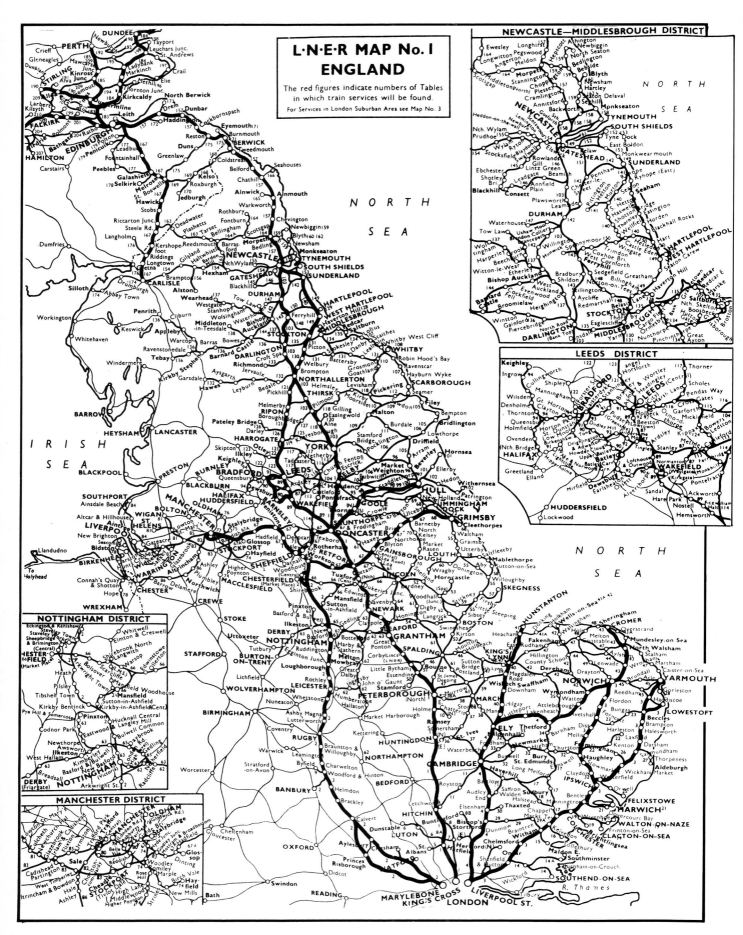

L·N·E·R MAP No. I
ENGLAND

The red figures indicate numbers of Tables
in which train services will be found.

For Services in London Suburban Area see Map No. 3

NEWCASTLE—MIDDLESBROUGH DISTRICT

LEEDS DISTRICT

NOTTINGHAM DISTRICT

MANCHESTER DISTRICT

now was to see them become a part of a unified transport system embracing road haulage and the canals. Hugh Dalton, then Chancellor of the Exchequer, said of them (in December 1946) that 'this railway system of ours is a very poor bag of physical assets. The permanent way is badly worn. The rolling stock is in a state of great dilapidation. The railways are a disgrace to the country.'

British Railways was duly born with all the hopes for a new beginning, a new golden age. It inherited 19,639 route miles (52,253 track miles), 20,148 locomotives, 40,257 passenger vehicles and 1,223,634 freight vehicles, and a very considerable number of horses. In the grey aftermath of a world war, of rationing and Korea, passenger traffic surged to new heights as the masses fought to get to the seaside for their newly-won summer holidays. Old and dilapidated rolling stock was hauled by old and dilapidated engines, and trains queued block-to-block on summer Saturdays. The railways creaked under the strain; new steam engines appeared from the old companies' works – and slowly but surely the decline set in, aggravated by material and labour shortages. Burgeoning personal prosperity ushered in the 'you never had it so good' era, and the relentless rise of the motor car and the

motor lorry remorselessly took their toll, aided and abetted by the ever-powerful roads lobby.

The initial organisation of the regions certainly reflected the LNER's position, although had the original ideas in the 1948 Transport Act – for complete integration of the different transport modes – been implemented, things might have turned out quite differently. As it was, a link with the past had been severed on 23 December 1950 when the LNER, Great Western and LMS companies were finally dissolved, the Southern having gone on 10 June 1949. In October 1951 Clement Atlee's Labour Government was replaced by Winston Churchill's Conservatives. There was great opposition from the Tories to the centralised control of transport, and it looked for a brief period as if the old companies were about to return. In the Transport Bill published on 9 July 1952, which passed into law in 1953, it was proposed to sell off the state-owned road haulage business, a move which was strongly opposed by the British Transport Commission. Another consequence of the new Act was the setting up of area boards for the railways, thus giving the regions greater day-to-day control, but also larger responsibilities for wider issues. Road transport was duly denationalised and deregulated, and the railways were

Above right:
'A3' No 60085 *Manna* is at the head of a Doncaster-Grantham local, in spite of the headcode; somewhat of a humble duty for a Pacific. Here it is running into Retford on 16 July.
J. Cupit

Right:
In August 1949 platform 9S at York station is host to North Eastern Railway Class D20 No E2361, which has arrived with a stopper from Doncaster.
Real Photographs K378

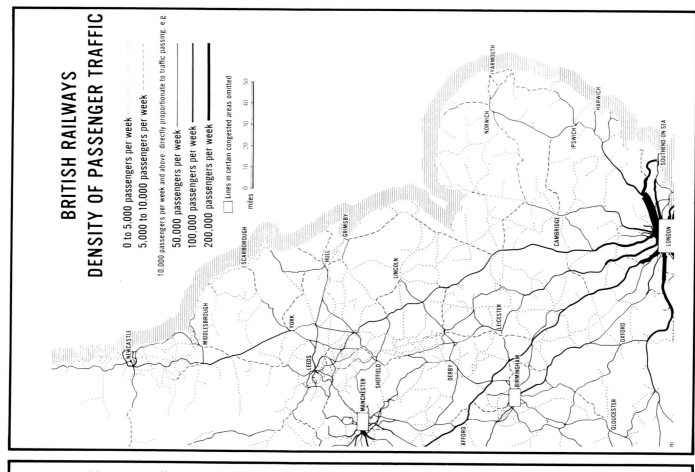

BRITISH RAILWAYS
DENSITY OF PASSENGER TRAFFIC

0 to 5,000 passengers per week
5,000 to 10,000 passengers per week
10,000 passengers per week and above: directly proportionate to traffic passing. e.g.
50,000 passengers per week
100,000 passengers per week
200,000 passengers per week

☐ Lines in certain congested areas omitted

miles 0 10 20 30 40 50

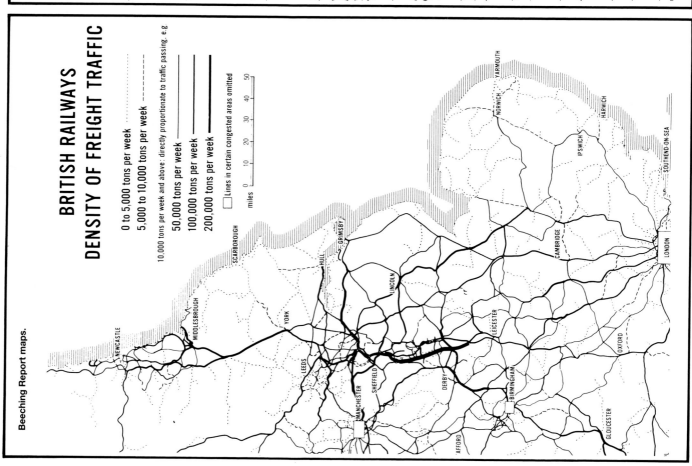

Beeching Report maps.

BRITISH RAILWAYS
DENSITY OF FREIGHT TRAFFIC

0 to 5,000 tons per week
5,000 to 10,000 tons per week
10,000 tons per week and above: directly proportionate to traffic passing. e.g.
50,000 tons per week
100,000 tons per week
200,000 tons per week

☐ Lines in certain congested areas omitted

miles 0 10 20 30 40 50

left to compete with the roads on unequal terms – just as the 'Big Four' had complained through their prewar 'Square Deal' campaign, and just as they were subsequently left to do.

British Railways responded to the falling traffic with the Modernisation Plan, designed to return them to profit, but seemingly not noticing that times were changing. Whilst many of its remedies were inspired – and the first generation diesel railcars were a lasting monument to their designers and builders – many failed to take account of the gathering pace of change. Many small diesel locomotives, built for the local pick-up goods trains of yesteryear were sold straight into industrial service, and never turned a wheel for British Railways. The deficits grew, and finally it was deemed that only surgery could save the patient from this haemorrhage. Enter Doctor Richard Beeching, appointed by a government whose Transport Minister had very recently been boss of a major road construction company.

To be fair, Dr Beeching was given a remit by the government, and as one of the most able businessmen of his day, carried it through with great efficiency. British Railways had been pursuing a policy of closing minor lines and withdrawing unremunerative services before he joined them: the Midland & Great Northern had closed in February 1959, and the Great Eastern's Beccles to Yarmouth main line followed in November. The North Eastern's branch from Kirkby Stephen to Tebay had closed in 1952, with the passenger service over the rest of the line, from Barnard Castle to Appleby and Penrith, going ten years later. Beeching also envisaged improvements in services with, for example, the advent of liner trains for freight. In the event, most of the lines that he proposed for closure duly had their services withdrawn: the Great Central's London extension, the East Lincs line of the former Great Northern, the Hornsea and Withernsea branches of the North Eastern being notable examples.

Some did survive his axe: Middlesbrough to Whitby, Harrogate to York, Skegness and the East Suffolk line being noteworthy survivors to this day. On the other hand, some lines survived Beeching and have since gone: March to Spalding, Wymondham to King's Lynn, Barkston to Lincoln and the Alnwick branch to name but a few. One bonus has been that many of the preserved lines which now abound could not have come into existence had Dr Beeching not closed them; notable within the Eastern and North Eastern Regions are the North Yorkshire Moors, Keighley & Worth Valley and Great Central lines. Others such as the North Norfolk are on lines that closed before he came along (although Sheringham to Melton Constable actually survived for passengers until 1964) – Dr Beeching tends to be blamed for a lot of things that he didn't do!

What of the events during the years between nationalisation and the arrival of the doctor? From the geography of the LNER's systems it clearly made sense to operate the lines in much the same way as under their pre-grouping ownership, so the Great Eastern lines out of Liverpool Street formed one unit, the Great Central line from Marylebone another, and the East Coast main line from King's Cross a third, and this was perpetuated in the initial operational organisation of British Railways. The LNER's relative poverty led to greater efficiency of working, and also to the prolongation of pre-grouping equipment and infrastructure, which was thus enabled to survive into the British Railways era. Most enthusiasts are familiar with North Eastern heavy freight locomotives such as the 'Q6s', or the little 'J27s', or the Great Eastern's 'J15s', or the GNR's 'A3s'; the Robinson 2-8-0s, originally of the Great Central, ended up almost everywhere, not just on former LNER lines. Even if it is only preserved examples that have led to that familiarity, the locomotives could not have

entered that state unless they had been very long-lived in the first place.

The express types did not survive so well, of course, since they were continually displaced by the very latest machines to emerge for front-line duty. By definition an engine that has raced along the main lines is unlikely to be suitable for secondary work on a branch line – it is probably much too heavy. Only the Great Northern could show 'Pacifics' surviving into the modern era, and that because Nigel Gresley had succeeded to the top job in the LNER from the same position with the GNR. Vincent Raven had produced some fine machines for the North Eastern, but it was the new standard engines of GNR derivation that replaced them.

British Railways' Eastern and North Eastern Regions thus inherited a mixed bag of stock – some up to the minute (allowing for the ravages of war) and some positively antediluvian. The stations were again a varied assortment. Some, such as York and Newcastle, had been large and well-designed and had served well. King's Cross was a fine design but had suffered encroachment from a variety of jumbled developments along its frontage. Peterborough was a major problem – two stations, and North an operational nightmare; Liverpool Street, in common with many others, had suffered serious bomb damage to its offices and to its roof, where all the glass had been removed for safe storage, but had got broken anyway. Some of the depots were in a truly dreadful state, especially on the Great Eastern, with cramped conditions, no mechanisation and poor layouts, and staff worked miracles under the circumstances.

The war had taken a heavy toll. The railways had been taken under central control by the Railway Executive, on which they were all represented, and in which officers from the companies played a major role. Very many staff had joined the armed forces, even though many railway jobs were reserved occupations, and women were often recruited to take their place. Vast quantities of extra war traffic (both in terms of passengers and freight) had been carried, in effect at no cost to the government, all of which had taken its toll of maintenance. Capital renewal had been put off: examples included electrification schemes on the Northern Heights branches in London, or Woodhead; widening of the main line from New Barnet northwards, from York northwards and so on; planned rebuilding of depots had not been done. The railways were indeed in a poor state, though they did not justify Dalton's slur, and were hardly recompensed for the pounding they had taken in the service of their country.

Not that they didn't plan for the future: on 26 July 1945 the LNER Board of Directors approved a postwar reconstruction programme showing measures of first and second priorities, each totalling £25 million. The money would come from renewals rendered unnecessary by the scheme, from deferred maintenance and from claims on the War Damage account, and generally a 5% return was expected. The exception to this was that improvements to the Company's homes for its staff were to be given top priority, and no return was expected, but the need was pressing. £3.75 million was allocated for the purpose. Expenditure on docks and electrification were excluded from the scheme, having been considered separately – for example, the board had already approved the rehabilitation of the steamships operating from Harwich Parkeston Quay. Examples of work in the 'first priority' category were the building of new depots at Colchester and Langwith, new offices at King's Cross, a new station at Peterborough North, widening from Greenwood to Potters Bar on the ECML, and also Pilmoor to Alne; resignalling of the Hatfield-Dunstable branch to cope with the heavy traffic from the many private sidings, new

loops at Rotherham, Tinsley East, Rugby and Beighton; rebuilding of Sunderland station at a cost of £250,000, also Middlesbrough, and the provision of modern refreshment rooms at Harrogate, Bridlington and York (amongst others), these three having been authorised in 1939.

This plan and its contemporaries from the other companies were doomed, however, for on 5 July 1945 the Labour Party swept to power with a manifesto commitment to integrate transport on a national scale. On 28 November 1946 the Transport Bill was introduced, which announced an intention to bring transport services generally under public control, and the railway companies banded together to fight the proposals. The LNER produced an alternative scheme which, with echoes of the current privatisation scheme, envisaged the selling to the State of the track and fixed assets in return for a lease to operate train services. Suffice it to say that the proposal did not find favour. The Bill was duly passed, and the Railway Executive was set up as a shadow organisation, taking over from the companies at midnight on 31 December 1947. The new British Railways was broadly organised into regions reflecting the former companies. Before long, adjustments started to be made to regional boundaries to tidy up some of the anomalies, such as those where lines of one company had penetrated the territory where another was dominant. This meant that some lines were in one region geographically, but in a different one operationally. For example, the Great Central main line from Marylebone to Manchester was to remain operated throughout by the Eastern Region, although from Marylebone to Northolt Junction it was geographically part of the Western, and the Woodhead route became London Midland. The seeds of its downfall were sown early by this confusion!

Nevertheless the outward appearances remained much the same at first. 'British Railways' appeared on the sides of engines instead of the initials of the LNER, and some rather odd liveries could be seen before the pattern settled down again. British Railways were part of a much larger undertaking – the British Trans-

port Commission (BTC) – which also included the inland waterways and roads, and it was the intention to provide an integrated system. It is well-known that new emblems, such as the 'cycling lion' and corresponding lettering were devised for the railways, but less widely appreciated that similar devices were also produced for the other modes of transport. In fact, there was a whole portfolio of approved material for use on all the Commission's undertakings.

Station gardens had been a feature of the railways for almost as long as they had existed. In the very early days of long hours, poor working conditions and pay it had been a necessity for many men to cultivate what land they could in order simply to survive, and the lineside allotment remains a feature today. Station gardens were perhaps born from this, and also from one of the essential features of country stations, which was that there would be furious bursts of activity when trains were about, punctuated by spells of quiet. There were competitions for the best kept gardens, with awards in no fewer than six categories: special class (£8), then first (£5), second (£4), third (£3) and fourth class (not in the North Eastern), and also 'Certificates of Commendation'; the amounts were those awarded on the North Eastern Region in 1955. In that year the Eastern Region distributed nearly £800 to its stations in prize money. The competition was run by the operating region, so that (for example) Appleby East, Kirkby Stephen East and Warcop all received North Eastern commendations, although they were geographically in the London Midland Region. Inspections and judging were typically made by retired officers using an inspection saloon and engine, so that on the North Eastern in 1955 the task was undertaken by Mr T. A. Wooding, a retired revenue accountant, and Mr H. R. Garth, retired Assistant Chief Civil Engineer at York. Displays were often elaborate and beautiful, with staff taking great pride in them, although the contrary view was also expressed by some, to the effect that it was all a dreadful waste of time and money.

To counter this on the North Eastern, Mr Burgis, stationmaster at Beverley in 1948, expressed the view that the station gardens competition (and its associated 'Best Kept Station' contest) gave the staff an incentive to take a personal pride in maintaining a high standard of appearance, as well as encouraging their supervisors to take more interest in their achievements. At Danby, stationmaster Jack Patterson felt that the appearance of stations had improved greatly with the re-introduction of the competitions since the war, and made them much more pleasant for the travelling public. It was also felt that this periodical inspection of stations helped to keep them up to scratch generally. Many staff also belonged to local allotments associations which existed to help members by bulk buying of seeds, fertilisers and the like, and to give advice on increasing crop yields, especially important in the days during and after the war when rationing was still in force.

Danby station, on the Middlesbrough-Whitby line between Battersby and Grosmont, aimed for a year-round display and had narrow borders between the platform and station buildings, with a plot about 60x5yd on the opposite side of the line, sloping up from a low stone wall to a privet hedge. Two large monkey puzzle trees stood, one at each end, with lawn at their base, and a plot of garden between. An astonishing variety of herbaceous plants was used, which were combined with hardy annuals to give a varied show year-on-year. Dahlias and begonias completed the display to give a splash of summer colour. At Monkseaton, a location where conditions could scarcely be more different, annuals were favoured since they would grow in poor soils and still give banks of colour. At Beverley, on the other hand, the display was deliberately arranged to be at its best in July and August, coinciding with the peak holiday traffic and also the judging in August. In 1960 the station won its sixth successive special award.

On the Eastern Region, two porters at Haverhill, S. Crow and R. Farrant, set about creating a garden in 1948, and managed to win awards every year: two thirds, two seconds and four firsts. They had taken a barren embankment and laid out lawns and flower beds, built walls, a rockery and a paved rose garden, and supplied tubs to the platform. Elsenham and Stansted were two others that were always up among the winners, and at both the staff raised plants in their own cold frames. An unlikely contender was Bethnal Green, where the staff started in Coronation Year with some old oil drums and soil from an embankment, later progressing to bulbs in tubs, using soil from Temple Mills. Staveley Central was another to put on a consistently fine display, winning one of only three special awards in 1956, and another in 1958. In that year 'Special' prizes were also won by Grimston Road and Sutton Bridge, with a first class for Hillington. They made sure that the M&GN went out on at least one high note – they had all been closed by the time the next awards were made.

The railways had also encouraged staff in various other departments by means of different awards. On the permanent way there was the competition for the 'Prize Length', with notices being displayed by the lineside. There were also awards for acts of gallantry, very often something that had averted an accident or prevented something worse. One day in 1948 at Sutton Bridge the 5.10am 'News' from Peterborough stopped short of the platform with the rear coach on fire. It pulled up so that it could be reached with the station hose-pipe, but the next coach caught fire, and with great difficulty because of the tight curve, shunter H. Tolliday and signalman L. R. Phillips managed to uncouple the two coaches and set them back. Tolliday phoned for the fire brigade, then played the hose on the station roof which was also now on fire, whilst Phillips got on with putting the fire out in the third coach of the train. Both received cash awards and letters of

commendation from the District Superintendent at Cambridge. On 9 July 1948 the right-hand injector blew out on Class V2 locomotive No 943, working an express fish train between Little Bytham and Essendine. Driver F. Barrett, of New England, told his fireman to ride on the step for safety, and managed to close the regulator and bring the train to a stand, despite being badly scalded. He then used a shunting pole to open the left-hand injector and so got the pressure down far enough to allow them to regain the footplate. Driver Barrett's award was made in the presence of local officials and trades union representatives by Mr J. Blundell, District Locomotive Superintendent at Peterborough.

In its early days the British Transport Commission was very conscious of the need to make good the ravages of war, but material shortages continued to make themselves felt. Although there was a surplus of nearly £8.5 million in 1952 (compared to £3 million in 1951) capital investment was severely limited to £76.6 million, and was estimated to be £6.8 million underspent, largely due to the shortage of steel, where the industry was still under government control. This shortfall was principally borne by the rolling stock programme, and it was necessary to repair stock that was forty or fifty years old. It was estimated that since 1949 £600,000 had been spent to extend its life by an average of four years. In 1952 the proportion of passenger stock awaiting repair rose from 6.9% in 1951 to 7.5%. Similar problems were experienced with goods stock, where the large numbers of old grease-lubricated wagons were slower and needed more frequent inspection.

On the positive side, trials of the new Automatic Warning System went ahead on the East Coast main line between New Barnet and Huntingdon, and plans were put in hand for the electrification to Chelmsford, and to Ipswich if possible. The British Transport Commission had pursued a policy of closing loss-making branch lines and stations, and disposing of other assets where it saw fit. Between 1948 and 1951 827.5 miles of line lost their passenger services, freight went from 259.75miles, both from 155.25 miles, making a total of 1,242.5 miles from which services had been withdrawn. Put another way, on lines still open 148 stations had lost their passenger services, 55 their goods and 31 both, and hotels were sold off at Leeds, Bradford and Felixstowe. The first fluorescent platform lights on British Railways appeared at stations between Liverpool Street and Shenfield in 1950, where they were parallel to the track on single-sided platforms, but at right-angles on islands, and carried on octagonal concrete columns 12ft 6in high spaced at 40ft intervals.

Fares and rates were increased in 1951 and gave a working surplus, but although in 1952 the first nine months were worked at a profit, the last three months of the year showed a loss. The problem was compounded by many factors, some out of the British Transport Commission's control. The Passenger Tribunal on fares, which had to arbitrate on charges, had given the BTC a rise of £4 million less than it needed. Government intervention on the fare increases, following public agitation, had cost a further £1.9 million. The cost of coal and steel to the commission had gone up to £7.5 million per annum, and additional fuel duty cost £5.5 million. The increase in National Insurance contributions cost a further £1.3 million, and together with wage increases brought about the loss in the last part of the year. 1952 saw the first revenue surplus (£2.9 million) under state control, and the revealing comment in the BTC Annual Report that 'the economies effected on the railways are all the more remarkable in view of the relatively small benefits (perhaps £800,000) derived from the closing of branch lines'. Many more small benefits were to come...

The East Coast floods early in 1953 did a great deal of damage. On the night of 31 January a combination of high tides and severe gales breached sea defences in many places, flooding or severing lines from Lincolnshire to the Thames estuary. Services to Cleethorpes were not fully restored until 8 February, but on the Mablethorpe-Willoughby branch it was much more serious. Trains of slag were brought in via Sutton-on-Sea to repair the yawning gaps in the line, but it was not until 2 March that services were resumed. The Downham-Lynn-Hunstanton route was flooded in several places, as was South Lynn, the line to Hunstanton being reopened after a week. The Wells-Heacham line was breached, but as passenger services had finished six months earlier, goods trains in future ran from either end. Just before 10pm water overflowed the north bank of Oulton Broad and flooded Lowestoft to a depth of 3ft, while at Yarmouth the south bank of Breydon Water burst, and South Town station – then being rebuilt – and the motive power depot were inundated. Shortly afterwards the north bank also went, and Vauxhall was flooded. The main line to London was breached at Belton and Aldeby, and there was severe damage to the line at Haddiscoe which took more than a fortnight to repair. The Harwich branch suffered damage in several places, although the Continental boat service was not interrupted. The London, Tilbury & Southend line – flooded to a depth of 10ft in places – was served by electric trains from Fenchurch Street to Shenfield – a section not normally seeing these units – thence steam to Southend Victoria. A three-mile stretch of the Brightlingsea branch was washed out, and it was not expected to survive the disaster; in the event it was rebuilt and reopened in December.

In 1953 the Railway Executive announced that it was aiming for a general increase in speed rather than simply running one or two very fast trains, although the Railway Magazine opined that 'high speed is not the attraction it was before air services were expanded'. Joseph Duddington, noted as the driver of Mallard when it broke the world record, died aged 76. The Railway Clearing House, set up in the early days of the private railway companies, had determined how revenue for the carriage of goods should be apportioned among them. It had become something of an anomaly with the nationalisation of the railways, they now being under the control of a single organisation, and it passed to the British Transport Commission on 24 May 1954. It continued to function from its offices in Eversholt Street, Euston until it was wound up in 1962.

Even before the Modernisation Plan, diesel railcars (later to be called multiple units) were being introduced on some services. In November of 1954, C. K. Bird, Eastern Region General Manager, called for steps to be taken to ensure that after the railcars had been in operation for some time, it would be possible broadly to compare their economics with those of the displaced steam services. Accordingly, two large-scale passenger censuses were arranged in 1955, one in the week ending 27 March and the other in the week ending 3 September. There were a few railcar services involved in the summer figures, but none in the winter. Revenue assessment was based on ticket types held by passengers, and parcels, mails and so on were excluded. Note of movement costs was taken, based on normal utilisation of engines, carriages and men, and also of the type and composition of the trains operated. About 40% of the stopping services on the Eastern Region were included in the census, together with a few fast and semi-fast services.

Summarising the results, the report noted that gross passenger receipts from steam stopping trains were £880,000, but that movement costs totalled £2,110,000, leaving a deficit of £1,230,000 and a costs/receipt ratio (or operating ratio) of 240%. However, an increase of about 20% in service levels on some routes in the summer was matched by revenue increases of some 150%, though the effect of this was reduced when spread throughout the year. An average of 11% of seats on stopping trains were first class (about 20 per train) though the average throughout-load was less than one passenger. Individual trains showed wide variations in loading, and low throughout-load factors sometimes masked full loadings for short distances. The results for the few diesel railcar services in operation at the time of the second census had to allow for the fact that services were often considerably increased with their introduction; nevertheless gross receipts were £2,100 and movement costs £1,600, giving a costs/receipt ratio of 73% – much better than the steam average, and better even than

Right:
Goathland, on the Malton to Whitby line, seen on 29 September 1962. The station won prizes for its gardens, such as the second class award of £4 in 1955.
Douglas Thompson

the best steam figure, which was 87%. (The worst of these, incidentally, was a staggering 935% on the Mildenhall branch!)

There had been concern at the British Transport Commission almost from its inception at the uneconomic nature of some stations and services, notably in the rural areas, and the results from this survey provided ample confirmation. As early as 1949 a report had been prepared which looked especially at the service between Ipswich and Norwich, which noted that there were 13 intermediate stations which (excluding Stowmarket and Diss) showed aggregated receipts of about £15,000 for passenger traffic and just under £5,000 for parcels and miscellaneous traffic. The report surmised that the cost of operating the stopping service exceeded its direct costs, and possibly the total traffic value of the stations. Whilst conceding that receipts from originating traffic were not necessarily a true index to the importance of the stations, the report also noted that there would be benefits to the operational efficiency of other passenger and freight working from the elimination of slow passenger trains. Interestingly enough, the first suggested remedy was the equalisation of road and rail fares (the BTC was operating under the 1947 Transport Act which proposed an integrated transport system), after which a fair assessment of the need for the local trains would be made. It felt that consideration should be given to the carrying of all passenger traffic from these stations by road.

The Norwich to Ipswich line was one of those chosen for the 1955 investigation, and all of its services (fast, semi-fast and stopping) were subject to the survey. In the March week the fast trains showed gross receipts of £1,710 and movement costs of £764, giving a ratio of 45%. The respective figures for the semi-fast service were £1,816, £1,758 and 97%, whilst for the stopping service they were £496, £1,752 and a disastrous 353%. Some other data from the census shed interesting light on operations at the time: the figures for train miles on the three types of service were fast 1,890, semi-fast 4,197 and stopping 3,780; for average number of vehicles per train fast 7.5, semi-fast 6.3 and stopping 4.1; for total passengers fast 227,835, semi-fast 276,106 and stopping 98,153; and over all load factors fast 37%, semi-fast 23% and stopping 13%. For the stopping services, dieselisation and the summer season improved matters slightly, so that the operating ratio improved to

a mere 323% and the load factor to 16%. The full report did not appear until 1956, by which time the stopping services on the line were dieselised.

With this sort of economics, the withdrawal of local trains seems inevitable, though the arguments about cost-cutting and marketing will undoubtedly continue. The railways were operating with Victorian technology and under a legal framework that had hamstrung them from the earliest days of the internal combustion engine. The local stations were still fully staffed, branches were fully signalled and the law did not permit the automation of level crossings. No serious attempt had yet been made to cut costs except by the occasional closure such as the Laxfield branch, and even where passenger services were withdrawn (as on the Eye or Hadleigh branches) a freight service continued and the infrastructure remained largely untouched. The writing was on the wall for local train services.

By 1955 the shortage of labour was making itself felt, especially in train manning, permanent way and shunting, and in the big cities such as London. The North Eastern Region organised two special careers display units which were sent to public and grammar schools in its area to try to recruit more staff. The speed and certainty of rail deliveries had declined and freight trains were being cancelled. On 19 March 1956 a national publicity campaign was launched to attract and retain staff for British Railways, and also to try to improve productivity. Passenger traffic fell in 1955 by 1.4% from the previous year, and passenger miles by 2%, in spite of the ASLEF strike. This had been called for midnight on Saturday 28 May and continued until Tuesday 14 June, and was settled by the 'Lord Justice Morris' award at a cost of £400,000 per annum. Traffic had diverted to road, especially fish from Hull and Grimsby, the strike also having coincided with a rise in rates. Supplies of coal had been maintained to public utilities, and contingency plans to run freight trains had given milk, fish, fruit and essential foodstuffs priority.

Diesel railcars were introduced by the end of June in Lincolnshire, on five more routes in Norfolk and Suffolk in September, and between Newcastle and Middlesbrough in November. The inaugural run of the 'Car Sleeper Ltd' between King's Cross and Scotland was on 19 June: there were two workings each way

Left:

A spacious station had been carved out of a difficult location, set deep down with high brick retaining walls and tunnels at each end; Nottingham Victoria looking towards the train shed in 1964.

Douglas Thompson

13

weekly, each of the first three down trains carrying the full complement of 20 cars. Third class fares were raised by 0.13d (0.05p) per mile in June, but remained below the authorised maximum of 2d (0.84p), so that British Railways' fares were now about double those of prewar days, although the cost of living had risen by 250%.

Freight also showed an overall fall. Ton-miles of minerals and steel by rail rose, but there was a decline in livestock and merchandise, with a considerable transfer of coal to the roads. The rail strike was one cause, but the main culprit was the 'C-licence', the number of which had shown a steady rise – up by 150% since 1938. It was estimated that using this system there were some 150,000 vehicles of up to 2.5 tons unladen weight (or more) running empty or less than half-loaded for half their time on the road. Operators of these vehicles could pick and choose their traffic, charge whatever rate they wanted and leave the railways, still under a legal obligation as common carriers, with the unremunerative flows. British Railways staff numbers fell by 14,414, but good progress had been made on the new yard at Temple Mills and on the colour-light resignalling at Newcastle Central. It was decided to standardise on 50Hz AC for electrification, and on the vacuum brake for other than multiple-unit stock. The rate of closure continued apace, another 39 stations losing their passenger services.

The Modernisation Plan was announced by the British Transport Commission in January of 1955, having been in preparation for a year. It was to cost £1,200 million over 15 years, with its main parts starting within five years, and with at least half its costs coming from maintenance and renewal that would have to be done anyway. It was aimed to exploit the natural advantages of the railway by concentrating on the activities it did best, by re-equipment and by transferring uneconomic services to road. Main line speeds of at least 100mph were envisaged, with associated track and signalling improvements; diesel and electric traction would replace steam, the two being seen as complementary. It was proposed to electrify the ECML to Doncaster, Leeds and possibly York, as well as the West Coast line from Euston to Birmingham, Crewe, Liverpool and Manchester, although it was recognised that one of the two might have to be dieselised as an interim measure, since that would avoid the heavy engineering costs of electrification. In the event, the ECML had to wait over thirty years, although the suburban sections were done sooner, and it did reach all the way to Edinburgh. Greater cleanliness was seen as a major benefit of the removal of steam traction, and much rebuilding of depots and stations was also envisaged in order to maximise this. It was also recognised that many of the benefits would appear only when a substantial amount had already been done, and steam eliminated completely from large areas. Continuous braking for all goods wagons was seen as another important way of speeding trains.

Prompted by the needs of the Modernisation Plan a number of committees were set up to examine particular issues. One was the 'Passenger Stations Group', which made its first report in March 1956, with echoes of the LNER's reconstruction plans of eleven years earlier. Among its 'first priority' stations were Peterborough North, where a £2 million reconstruction would provide a new central station and running facilities, and eliminate the severe speed restrictions, since the present station was considered inadequate for traffic requirements. Parkeston Quay station was to be reconstructed at no outlay in connection with improvements to the packet port terminal. On the 'second priority' list were Colchester, where alterations to the layout in connection with the Ipswich electrification were contemplated; modernisation of Liv-

erpool Street at a cost of £3.5 million; lengthening of platforms, revision of signalling and new running facilities at Ipswich; reconstruction of Cambridge and Lincoln stations with extra platforms at a cost of £1.5 million and £0.5 million respectively, and enlargement of facilities at either Yarmouth Vauxhall or Beach, at a cost of £0.5 million in connection with the possible rearrangement of local and long-distance working.

The 'Traffic Survey Group' was another set up under the Modernisation Plan to exploit the advantages of rail in bulk transport and to maximise efficiency, and their remit pointed inexorably towards block or liner trains. They noted that 60% of stations handled less than 20 wagons per week, and that the journeys involved tripping to or from marshalling yards at either end. There were delays in yards and on the running lines, and cancellations due to inadequate motive power, which all led to poor service and high costs. However, the group also recognised that the loss of stations might disadvantage the railways; it liked the conventional 10T container and wanted to introduce the 'piggy-back' system. It didn't, somewhat strangely, see a reduction in need for marshalling yards – just the need to site them more carefully. It wanted train speeds increased so that all trains on a line would run at the same speed for greater economy and efficiency, and a rise in parcels rates to an economic level, together with their transfer to express freight trains: they made unsightly piles on platforms!

The abolition of third class was announced at the start of 1956, to take place from 3 June. Second class had been available only on boat trains in recent years, and then only so that uniformity could be maintained with continental railways. With this in mind it was to be completely withdrawn, and third renamed second, since the European railways were also adopting a similar two-class policy. When the change was actually implemented there was little visible alteration, with temporary signs employed and old ticket stocks continuing to be used until replacement was required. Another outward change that was phased in gradually was that of the emblem: the old 'cycling lion' was replaced with a new version. It showed a 'demi-lion rampant' holding a silver locomotive wheel, the lion being issuant from a heraldic crown of gold on which were arranged a rose, thistle, leek and oak leaves, representing England, Scotland, Wales and Great Britain as a whole. It was designed in conjunction with Dr C. A. H. Franklin, and was approved by the College of Arms (England) and the Lyon Court (Scotland). The first locomotive to carry the device was No 70016 *Ariel*.

The Modernisation Plan had been expected to cover the 15 years between 1955 and 1970, and would return the railways to profitability. It acknowledged the human needs involved, but that didn't stop the increasing pace of closures. The Midland & Great Northern system was the first major amputation, and was to see 189 miles go at a stroke, with an estimated annual saving of £640,000. The Eastern Region board had submitted closure proposals to the East Anglian and East Midlands Transport Users' Consultative Committees (TUCCs), who had received representations from 4 county councils, 1 county borough, 6 urban district councils, 16 rural district councils, 23 parish councils and other associations of local authorities, chambers of trade and commerce and many other bodies, as well as a number of private firms and individuals. In spite of this weight of protest and a number of counter-proposals the Eastern Region's plans were confirmed by the Central Transport Consultative Committee (CTCC) on 25 November 1958, which meant that the whole matter had been dealt with in only ten weeks. The CTCC congratulated all concerned on this! The closure duly took place on 28 February 1959,

Above:
A period piece at Bury St Edmunds as LMS-designed Class 2 No 46494 runs in with a short pick-up freight from Sudbury in May 1961. Although the branches and much of the track have now been removed from the station, the fine building has very recently undergone extensive renovation.
John C. Baker

the full service being maintained to the end. A few parts remained open, such as Sheringham to Melton Constable, and the lines between Gayton Road and East Rudham, and Norwich City and Melton Constable were retained for freight. The M&GN Preservation Society was formed almost at once to reopen the section between North Walsham and Yarmouth Beach, and had it been successful, intended to open a museum at the latter and to reopen other sections of line.

One other event of 1958 which should not go unrecorded is the death on the last evening of February of C. K. Bird, who had retired as Eastern Region General Manager on 31 January through ill-health. He had been a man of great ability who had led the Eastern well, and he was replaced by H. C. Johnson, later to become BR Chairman.

One of the features of British Railways in the pre-Beeching years was camping coaches. In 1958 there were over 200 at 125 sites, and they were available to let from the end of March to the end of October. They had sleeping accommodation for four, six or eight people, with a living room and well-equipped kitchen, and cooking utensils, crockery, cutlery, towels, table and bed-linen were provided. Bookings could be made for one or two weeks, the weekly rental ranging from £5 10s (£5.50) to £12 10s (£12.50) according to site and season, with prospective tenants having to buy a specified minimum number of rail tickets from their home station to that nearest the coach. On the North Eastern Region other accommodation was also available in converted station buildings on disused branches.

The 1959 timetable was complicated by the fact that there was a printing strike, and it proved impossible to issue the winter timetable on the due date. The summer one therefore continued in force, being extended from 13 September to 2 November, although with many of the summer extras removed.

Railway finances were becoming the cause of a great many headaches. The British Transport Commission had introduced 'deficit borrowing' in 1956, its finances having been in balance until 1955. Part of the blame for the deficit was put on the slowness of getting authority to raise rates, which then did not increase sufficiently. In 1958 there had been a severe recession in

coal and steel carrying, and in 1960 the threat of strike action by the NUR over pay. This was settled by the Guillebaud report, but at an annual cost of £33 million to the railway. Parliament had had the Modernisation Plan under almost continuous review since its inception, one reason being the need to maintain financial support for the railways. Early in 1959, for example, the 'Transport (Borrowing Powers) Bill' occasioned debate on the matter, it no longer being felt that BR would break even by 1962, and this bill increased the railway's borrowing limit from £600 million to £1,200 million. It emerged that the cost of stopping a train of four vehicles at a small station in Suffolk was 1s 4d (7p), mainly due to wear and tear on brakes, the cost being less if the train were a one- or two-car diesel multiple unit. It was very expensive to stop large trains, but the loss of goodwill if railcar stops were omitted was not worth the cost saving. Operating costs were also temporarily increased by the continuation of a mixed steam and diesel railway, but there was also the first recognition by a parliamentary select committee that it might be necessary to provide financial support for socially-necessary services. Staffing was still difficult because general full employment, high national wage rates, unsocial hours and poor working conditions made railway work unattractive.

Another significant policy decision with a long-term effect on the travelling public was taken early in 1958, and that was to discontinue the building of compartment coaches after completion of the year's programme. Much controversy was aroused which illuminated the letter pages of the press, it being considered that the loss of privacy would discourage travellers; until now open stock had generally been used only for excursions. Smoking also reared its head as an issue the following year. When the railways started it had been widely banned, and had found favour only in relatively recent years, compartments being labelled as 'Smoking' where it was permitted, rather than the reverse. By 1959 the tide was beginning to turn against it, with concern about the health implications becoming more widespread. London Transport had estimated that more than two-thirds of passengers did not smoke, and so (rather curiously) concluded that an equal number of smoking and non-smoking carriages on every train should suffice. On British Railways about one-fifth of accommodation at the time was non-smoking.

Progress was being made in the delivery of diesel multiple units, 3,694 being delivered by the end of 1960 out of a total of 4,110 ordered, which included the Blue Pullmans. In addition, 837 diesel locomotives had been delivered, and the last three steam locomotives had been built for British Railways. Over 2,000 coaches had been delivered during the year, and new vehicles for the future would incorporate features from the 1957 experimental stock. Express freight stock was almost all vacuum-fitted, and there were now 900 daily express goods services. Disc brakes were being tried out on 62 21-ton coal wagons, and Presflos had been introduced. Two prototype road-railers were on trial, having a payload of 11 tons, tare 5 tons; 50 had been ordered, to gain experience.

To counterbalance this modernity, it was not widely appreciated that British Railways took over very large numbers of horses in 1948, and that much of the shunting in small yards up and down the country was performed by these sturdy beasts: in some of the byways of East Anglia they survived into the 1960s. At Cambridge Goods station Boxer, a bay gelding, had arrived in 1945 aged 8, and retired on 8 January 1957. In 1961 Tiny Tim (aged 15) and Tommy (aged 21) were still performing their duties at Newmarket, a most appropriate place, and in October of that year Tommy took part in the 'Horse of the Year' show at Wembley. According to Mr Alfred Newton, his regular driver, he 'steps over rails and crossing points while hauling a heavy load. He does this with a practised nonchalance.' Tommy would not attempt more than two horse boxes, but if Mr Newton rattled the coupling links Tommy thought that one had been removed! He was an inveterate scrounger and would beg from women with shopping bags whilst waiting at the level crossing for a train. He also went looking for titbits from the kitchen cars of race trains stabled in the sidings – and was rarely disappointed! At Woodbridge the sleepers in the sidings were specially covered with gravel to assist the horses, and two of them could move three wagons there, although they were also allowed out on to the main line.

This was the railway scene on to which Dr Richard Beeching emerged. At the same time there was yet another reorganisation, and the British Transport Commission gave way to the British Railways Board, Dr Beeching being its first chairman. The impact of his 'Reshaping of British Railways' report, published on 27 March 1963 was widespread and in many ways devastating, large swathes of Britain losing their railways as a result. On the other hand it can be argued that he saved the network from greater disaster; it is quite certain that the effects of his tenure of office are still felt strongly today.

Let us now look at the various parts of the Eastern and North Eastern Regions in the years between nationalisation in 1948 and Dr Beeching's arrival in 1962.

Below:
A Derby Lightweight DMU pulls out of Leeds Central bound for Harrogate, whilst LNER Class J50 No 68984 pauses during shunting.
K. Field

CHAPTER

1 The East Coast Main Line

The East Coast Main Line dated back as an entity to the early days of the railways in Britain. Envisaged as a high-speed long-distance link, it was owned in the days of the great pre-grouping companies by three of them, the Great Northern, North Eastern and North British Railways. The ECML extended for 268.5 miles between King's Cross and Newcastle, with Berwick – the furthest outpost of the North Eastern – another 67 miles beyond. The route had had a complex history, with various changes and diversions as it developed, but cooperation between the three companies had been established at an early stage, urged on by the rivalry with the West Coast route of the London & North Western and Caledonian Railways. This resulted in the formation of the East Coast Joint stock fleet from 1860, taken into the LNER at the Grouping.

The Great Northern section of the ECML ran from King's Cross – a station whose road approaches and general appearance had been marred by uncontrolled development – through the northern suburbs of London and on to Peterborough, Grantham

and Doncaster before joining the North Eastern at Shaftholme Junction. The North Eastern part extended thence to Berwick serving York, Durham, Darlington and Newcastle, although the section from Shaftholme Junction to York did not open until 1871, trains having previously run via Knottingley. Further north the 'old main line' ran from Ferryhill to Gateshead via Leamside and Washington and retained its status until 1872 when the Team Valley route via Durham opened for through traffic. Even so, these earlier routes remained useful as diversions, and at times (such as the disastrous floods of 11-12 August 1948) other much smaller branches were pressed into such use.

Below:
The exterior of King's Cross station in September 1963. The fine uncluttered frontage was marred by the piecemeal development; note the original Metropolitan Railway building on the right.
Real Photographs K6059

The North British parts of the ECML are beyond the scope of this book; suffice it to say that NBR engines had not regularly worked south of Berwick, nor on the express trains on the ECML since the North Eastern had exercised its running powers to Edinburgh. In LNER days Nigel Gresley's introduction of new express locomotives such as the 'A3s' had allowed much greater efficiency of working as well as offering better journey times, and they had started working through between London and Edinburgh instead of being changed at York.

King's Cross station was, of course, the gateway to the East Coast main line, and celebrated its centenary in 1952. Opened on 14 October 1852 it replaced the Great Northern's temporary terminus at nearby Maiden Lane, and at 10 acres was the largest station in the country, with a magnificent roof. It was designed by Lewis Cubitt, cost £123,500 to build and an additional £65,000 for the purchase and removal of smallpox and fever hospitals once on the site. Unfortunately, by 1952 its imposing frontage had become marred by a cluster of buildings known colloquially as the 'African Village', although it had expanded with the addition of many more platforms, especially on the suburban side. The clutter was swept away when the Great Northern suburban electrification scheme was brought in and its appearance much enhanced as a result.

The front of the station was formed by two main arches with a span of 71ft, which marked the ends of the original arrival and departure platforms, and which were separated by the clock tower some 112ft high. When first built the clock struck, having three bells, but was silenced during World War 1, and after 1927 permanently. Traffic expanded rapidly, necessitating extensions to the station, including provision of the local platforms on the west side, and for the connections to the Metropolitan. Extra tunnels were built and eventually Maiden Lane (later Gasworks) and Copenhagen tunnels were triplicated and the flat junctions at Belle Isle eliminated.

In 1895 the local station was rebuilt, being modernised in 1938-9 and remained largely unchanged until completely remodelled for electrification. Track circuits had been introduced at King's Cross long before the term itself was coined (the Great

Above right:
King's Cross station in 1957 looking towards both the suburban and main line sections, across the turntable. Locomotives visible include 'N2' No 69521, 'B2' No 61632 and 'L1' No 67745.
N. C. Simmons

Right:
The interior of King's Cross in July 1961, with Grantham 'A3' No 60046 *Diamond Jubilee* heading a recent arrival in platform 2.
A. W. Flowers

Northern called them 'insulated rails') and colour light signalling and electric point motors were introduced in 1932, when the old East and West signalboxes were replaced by a single cabin. Platform alterations in the 1930s saw No 4 extended the full length of the station, with No 3 abolished; Nos 7 and 8 were widened to 24ft. No 10, the old departure platform, was nearly 1,000ft long and housed almost all the public offices and rooms. In 1936 new enquiry and seat reservation offices were opened, the buffet and restaurant enlarged and a tea-room added. A new uniform barrier was provided with illuminated platform numbers; LNER standard 'Gill-sans' lettering was adopted throughout.

The main office block was hit by a bomb on 11 May 1941, which also caused part of the main roof to collapse, being rebuilt in 1947. On 28 September 1952 a special train was run from King's Cross to York to mark the centenary of the terminal's opening, and also of the opening of the direct Werrington-Retford line on 14 October 1852. Hauled by 'A4' No 60007 *Sir Nigel Gresley*, it ran out via the direct line, and back via the old, at a fare of 35s per head, one of the ticket sellers being a Mr A. F. Pegler. An exhibition was also held at King's Cross from 13-18 October to celebrate its centenary.

King's Cross itself had many operational aspects. The station could be divided into the main line side and the suburban side, with the platform at York Road for trains serving the widened lines. The latter has long gone, swept away by the Thameslink scheme, and the suburban side is much reduced. Then there was the goods depot, a vast collection of sidings and sheds mostly on the down side, and the legendary 'Top Shed' – 34A in British Railways days. The main station was a simple and imposing structure, but the exit for trains was difficult, with a complex throat leading almost immediately to the fierce 1 in 107 climb out through Gas Works and then Copenhagen tunnels. Six tracks were fed through three sets of tunnels at each place, and apart from a brief respite through Hornsey, it was a steady uphill slog at 1 in 200 over the Northern Heights as far as Potters Bar.

Meantime Finsbury Park, at 2.5 miles from King's Cross, was a busy place. It saw connections with the North London line via Canonbury, and passenger services ran out on to the Great Northern from Broad Street, usually to Hertford North or Hatfield, although a few terminated intermediately. The Northern Line ran to Finsbury Park, and it had once been intended to use the surface station; in the event it had to make do with an underground terminus which was eventually taken over by the Victoria Line, and the connection, once intended to get trains from Moorgate to Alexandra Palace, did not materialise until British Rail took over from London Transport in the 1970s. The branches to Alexandra Palace, Edgware and High Barnet also fed in to Finsbury Park, which was also the focus for a number of important goods yards, notably Highbury Vale, Ashburton Grove and Clarence Yard; there were further sidings at Ferme Park and Harringay, and of course, the loco shed at Hornsey. At Harringay West Junction the single track connection from the Tottenham & Hampstead line trailed in on the down side, limited to 15mph, and invaluable for goods traffic.

Continuing northwards towards Wood Green the Hertford loop diverged to the east, a flyover carrying the down loop over the main line. There was a connection between the Palace Gates branch and the Great Northern at Bounds Green (now occupied by the InterCity depot) which was a useful interchange with the Great Eastern system, especially in the war years. The Hertford loop was not completed until December 1920, and was regarded by the Great Northern as relief for the main line, which could not easily be widened, especially between Welwyn and Woolmer Green, and for this reason the quadrupling of later years was put off. It was often used for diversions when engineering work was in progress on the main line, and the distance between Wood Green and Langley Junction (Stevenage) was only marginally longer than via Welwyn. Considerable suburban traffic developed over the loop, with some trains terminating at Gordon Hill. The building of the line had necessitated a new station at Hertford North, and was distinguished by passing through Ponsbourne tunnel, longest on the Great Northern. The old terminus (Cowbridge) of the branch from Welwyn was turned over to goods and parcels. Although it was a through station in layout it saw practically no passenger trains north-wards in the 1950s, the service to Stevenage and Hitchin having been suspended soon after the out-

Below:
'N2/2' No 69540 lifts a motley assortment of empty stock up Holloway bank on 9 May 1954. The signal gantry is interesting, as are the finely-cultivated allotments behind the train.
A. R. Carpenter

Right:

**No 60139 *Sea Eagle* heads the
down 'Flying Scotsman' up the
bank between the tunnels out of
King's Cross, past Goods & Mineral
Junction box. The North London
line crosses by the bridge ahead.**
Eric Treacy

break of war in 1939. The line onward to Langley Junction saw only goods traffic on a regular basis. Hertford North saw many more passengers than East, even after the latter had been electrified, probably because it offered a journey into London that was over five miles shorter.

The last of the various relief lines that had accompanied the four tracks of the main line finally finished at Wood Green No 2 box, which like many of the others near London on the ECML signalled either the up or the down lines (in this case, the up). Just beyond the station lay Wood Green tunnel (705yd), and then New Southgate station set in a deep cutting and approached past the giant STC works. Barnet tunnel (605yd) and Oakleigh Park station followed, and then New Barnet, which had been the end of the quadruple track section until the widening scheme of the 1950s. This again was typical of the suburban stations at the London end of the ECML, with carriage roads and shelters on its approaches, a long wide covered footbridge leading to a spacious wooden booking office over the tracks, with island platforms reached down covered sets of stairs. Little is now left of these: Wood Green, Hornsey and Harringay succumbed to the electrification and its associated rebuilding; New Southgate burnt down in the late 1970s; and New Barnet has since had a Network SouthEast rebuilding also after a major fire.

The ECML was scheduled to become a trial ground for the new British Railways standard type of Automatic Train Control early in 1950 when the apparatus was installed between New Barnet and Huntingdon, and both Pacifics and 'V2s' were fitted for the purpose. However, the first tests did not actually take place until 17 October 1952, when 'A1' No 60130 *Kestrel*, of Grantham shed, took the 3.10pm King's Cross to Edinburgh. The 'clear' indication was a bell and 'caution' a horn, and this system eventually spread to most parts of the railway.

In mid-1952 the scheme for widening the line between New Barnet and Potters Bar was being mooted. Contracts were let for the new tunnels at Potters Bar and Hadley Wood and the track needed, and for rebuilding of the station at Hadley Wood. By August 1955 the rebuilding of Potters Bar station was complete, with new island platforms and buildings at track level, together

with a new signal box. September saw the completion of the quadrupling between Greenwood and Potters Bar, which then provided four tracks all the way from King's Cross to Welwyn viaduct, a distance of 21 miles. Other works were scheduled for Arlesey, Sandy and the Huntingdon to Yaxley section, which would then have mean that four tracks were available all the way from King's Cross to Stoke summit (except for Welwyn tunnel and viaduct, which had proved insuperable obstacles), a distance of around 100 miles.

Potters Bar (marking almost the northernmost boundary of Middlesex until the reorganisation of 1974 moved it into Hertfordshire) was one of the first stations to be rebuilt as part of the modernisation plan. It took three years' work, until November 1955, and incorporated a number of novel features. Passenger facilities were housed in a combined booking and enquiry office – forerunner of today's travel centres – which also handled parcels traffic and left luggage. Two island platforms were provided, each with modern waiting shelters and canopies, and featuring minimal-maintenance finishes. The new signalbox, on the up side at the country end of the station, featured the first installation of a route-setting relay interlocking panel on which routes were set up and signalled on a 'geographical' basis. This meant (as with today's power installations) that the signalman operated the appropriate switches on the track diagram on the control console, and the points were moved and locked and the signals cleared. It had the advantage that it was unnecessary to remember all the switches that would otherwise be needed to set up a route, all that was needed being to set the switches at the entry and exit of a section of line. It was worked on the track-circuit block system.

The line then fell through Brookmans Park and Hatfield, and the latter was the terminus of many suburban services before the growth of Welwyn Garden City made it a more attractive objective. Small cross-country branches wandered off from here to Hertford, Dunstable and St Albans. Welwyn Garden City had been built to serve the new settlement, and became a terminus for outer suburban services. Immediately after the war many were still going through to Hitchin, but by 1951 many trains were starting or finishing at Welwyn, or running fast thence and then calling at Welwyn North, Knebworth and Stevenage to Hitchin. Some of the Cambridge trains also did this, but the buffet car expresses – the 'beer trains' – called only at Welwyn Garden City and Hitchin. At Hitchin the Cambridge line diverged to the east, and there were extensive yards, as well as apparatus for collecting and delivering mailbags to Travelling Post Offices on the move. There were also several sidings in the area – as in many other places – where the rules prohibited their use in the dark, or in fog or falling snow: the signals could not clearly be seen because there were no lamps in them.

Stevenage had been a relatively small town on both the Great North Road and the East Coast main line, with a population of some 7,000 in 1946. However, it had been designated under the New Towns Act of 1946 to grow to 60,000 with a new industrial area providing work for 12,000 people. Under the 1952 timetable it saw 51 trains a day, as well as generating considerable goods traffic from engineering products and soap. In order to cope with the projected growth of the town a new central railway and bus station were envisaged, together with a helicopter park! The old station, located in a cutting somewhat to the north of the present one, had a building of white brick with red relief on the up side at road level, from which a covered footbridge and stairs gave access to the platforms. On the up side of the station were Langley troughs and junction, and all engines travelling on the up main

were required to fill their tanks in order to avoid having to take water in London. Similarly, trains on the down main for Cambridge were also required to fill up here.

From Stevenage the line fell almost without interruption to Offord, three miles from Huntingdon, and even then rose only gently before falling through Abbotts Ripton, grazing the edge of East Anglia as it passed dead level through Holme, and then on to Peterborough. Biggleswade, Sandy and St Neots were busy and important towns, although some of the other stations on the section closed in the 1950s; Arlesey has since reopened on a different site. Biggleswade station benefited from its being on one of the four-track sections, and it had two island platforms with a spacious goods yard able to accommodate 500 wagons. It was a railhead and handled zonal traffic with its fleet of road motors, and was also a sack concentration depot for various firms, hiring out over 500,000 every year. A great deal of sugar beet was handled for forwarding to the refinery at Peterborough, and to cap it all it won a succession of first class awards in the annual station gardens competition in the late 1940s and early 1950s.

Huntingdon had a connection for the Great Northern & Great Eastern Joint line to St Ives, although its trains served the East station, as opposed to North, on the main line. Holme was the junction for the 5.75 mile branch to Ramsey North (the connection to Ramsey East was mooted but never made), which boasted

Above left:
An up freight train is seen emerging from the tunnel at Hadley Wood on Sunday 13 July 1952, headed by Class B1 No 61027 *Madoqua*. Permanent Way work is in progress, but high-visibility clothing has not yet been introduced.
B. E. Morrison

Left:
Work is in full swing on the quadrupling of the main line at Hadley Wood on 14 July 1958. The new platforms and tunnel at the north end have been built, and a narrow gauge railway is being used to transport materials around the site.
British Railways

only three passenger trains each way in 1946 and was withdrawn in 1947, although it survived for goods as late as 1973.

Peterborough has long been a major railway centre, although the Great Northern line was a relative latecomer. The Great Eastern line from March brought considerable traffic from East Anglia, but used the East station, as did the London Midland (formerly LNWR) trains to Market Harborough and Northampton, and the former Midland trains to Leicester. However, the Midland & Great Northern served the North station, and some of the Leicester trains also called there. A shuttle was also provided to link the two, although there could be considerable inconvenience to travellers who wanted to change between stations. Until 1982, of course, Peterborough was not the inevitable focus of all trains from East Anglia, as many services could and did take the GN&GE Joint line between March, Spalding, Lincoln and Doncaster, and for the same reason, the yards at New England and elsewhere did not have the same importance: Whitemoor (March) was the obvious place to remarshal traffic and have the major locomotive depot for freight work.

Peterborough North managed to compound the problems by having a very severe speed restriction due to the track curvature through the station. This was as low as 20mph in the years immediately following the war, and its effect on the running of express trains was severe. Because of the tight curvature, plungers were provided on both the up main (No 2) and down main (No 3) platforms so that guards could advise drivers that their train was ready to start. A second plunger halfway along the platform allowed for short trains! Assistance was allowed for heavy trains in the down direction by an engine not attached to the rear of the train, which could go as far as the end of the station before dropping off.

Proposals were put forward in 1956, as part of the new Modernisation Plan, for its reconstruction as part of a scheme to provide a new central station, the cost being given as £2 million. The problem was finally removed only by the complete rebuilding in

Below:
Welwyn Garden City station in June 1951 is host to 'N7' 69695 on a local train.
Real Photographs K1139

the 1970s prior to the introduction of high speed services, initially provided by the 'Deltics' and later by InterCity 125s; at the same time, multiple-aspect signalling was introduced. This in itself represented a huge change in the railway scene: in the Peterborough area immediately after the war, there were mechanical signalboxes at (from the south) Fletton Junction, Crescent Junction, Peterborough North, Spital Junction, Westwood Junction, Eastfield, New England South, East and North, Walton and Werrington Junction; then there were all those on the Great Eastern and Midland, including Peterborough East, Fletton Road, Nene Junction and Spital Bridge – and that doesn't cover nearly all of them.

The Peterborough area was well known for its bricks, and several stations, yards and sidings had facilities for handling this extensive traffic. Yaxley had brick sidings, there were more at Haddon Road crossing about a mile to the north, and Fletton had extensive facilities, as might be expected. Fletton Junction provided a connection from the ECML to the LNWR line at Longueville Junction, the line being known as the Botolph branch, which could be used for stabling wagons of empties when needed. The London Brick Company and Forder's both had yards at Fletton which were served by a tramline; this was used for taking unfired bricks from the press sheds to the kilns and crossed the brick sidings by two swing bridges. Shunters had special instructions regarding these bridges, which had to be swung clear of the sidings, clamped and locked before shunting commenced.

Northwards from Peterborough the main line undulated gently, but with a level stretch of over two miles around Werrington, where the Spalding line diverged to the east, and where there were water troughs on the main line. From Helpston, where the Midland line diverged to the west towards Stamford and Leicester it started to climb, gently at first through Essendine, and then steepening through Little Bytham, Corby and on to the summit at Stoke. This, of course, was one of the great racing grounds of the Great Northern, and was the scene of Mallard's famous attempt on the world speed record for steam, when it achieved 125mph down Stoke Bank. (The LNER claimed only 125mph – the figure of 126mph seems to have arisen later, although it is the one that appeared on the commemorative plaque on the locomotive). Essendine station, in the middle of this racing ground, was the

Left:
An up Cambridge-King's Cross stopping train crosses Welwyn viaduct on 14 April 1953, headed by Class B1 No 61099. The station and south tunnel are in the background.
R. E. Vincent

Below:
'A1' Pacific No 60157 *Great Eastern* heads the down 'Tyne-Tees Pullman' north of Welwyn in July 1958. This train left King's Cross at 4.50pm and served York, Darlington and Newcastle only, with a supplementary second class single fare of 7s 6d (37½p) for the full distance.
Locomotive Publishing Co 24501

junction for two very minor branches, to Bourne and Sleaford to the north, and Stamford to the south; both lost their services at a relatively early date (June 1951 and June 1959 respectively), Essendine itself closing with the Stamford branch.

Little Bytham is perhaps better known to enthusiasts as the true starting point of the M&GN, although the station of that name was actually on the ECML, with the Midland crossing just to the north by an overbridge. The end-on junction with the M&GN was just to the east of this bridge, and there was no railway connection with the main line. The ECML swept onwards, through Corby Glen (renamed from Corby in 1947) and over the summit, down through Stoke tunnel (880yd). At Highdyke, about 1.25 miles from Stoke, the branch from Sproxton and Stainby joined the main line on the down side; it also fed in traffic from the Colsterworth mines, and closed in 1966.

On to Grantham, with its statue of Sir Isaac Newton in commemoration of the town's most celebrated son, where the station was on a sweeping curve. Trains for Nottingham used the outer face of the down platform, and there were also services to Lincoln and Sleaford, although the actual junction for these lines was at Barkston, some 4.5 miles to the north. Grantham was an important point operationally, and for many years major trains might call there instead of Peterborough. Its locomotive shed (35B), on the down side, was more important in terms of express working than Peterborough (35A), and hosted a significant allocation of Pacifics, mostly 'A3s', right up to the end of steam. Operationally that station presented some problems, partly because it was on a curve, which affected up trains particularly, and also because of the gradient, rising towards London (although there was a very short level section immediately south of the station). Heavy trains in either direction were allowed to be assisted by an engine in the rear – but not attached – for approximately two coach lengths only 'in order to provide initial impetus'. The taking of water also presented problems since the platform was relatively short: in the up direction, 'Pacifics' on express duties needing water had to give one crow passing Barrowby Road, whereupon a message would be passed on for the Grantham Yard up home signal to be cleared so that the locomotive could draw up far enough. Goods trains were strongly discouraged from taking water at Grantham passenger station, and arrangements were in force for it to be taken instead at Spittlegate Bridge, controlled by the Yard box. An up freight wanting water in this way would have to give two crows passing Barkston South Junction box.

For down trains Peascliffe tunnel intervened before Barkston was reached. This station closed in March 1955, having enjoyed the sparsest of services. In the 1951-2 winter timetable no branch trains were booked to call, either from Lincoln or Sleaford; otherwise one could travel to Grantham at 8.54am, arriving back at 12.53pm. If travelling in the other direction, however, an overnight stay would have been needed! The junctions were interesting, since the Nottingham-Sleaford line passed under the ECML just to the north of the station, there being connections towards Sleaford from both directions. This direct line was used by some excursion traffic, notably from Leicester Belgrave Road to destinations such as Mablethorpe and Skegness, and allowed such trains to avoid Grantham and the consequent reversal.

The main line continued to drop through Hougham and Claypole (Hougham was served only by the same trains as Barkston, but Claypole had an extra one in each direction!) both stations closing on 16 September 1957. At Newark South junction the line from Bottesford trailed in on the down side, also providing a connection from the GN&LNW joint line, and thus from Market Harborough and Leicester Belgrave Road. Newark station was

less than a quarter of a mile from the junction and had an up relief road, as well as a down loop and bay platform, granary and cattle docks. North signalbox was again less than a quarter of a mile further, and a further half mile was the notorious level crossing over the Midland's Lincoln-Nottingham line. Unfortunately for the Great Northern the Midland was there first, and so its trains had precedence over those on the ECML.

Newark's Northgate station lies exactly 120 miles from King's Cross. It was a relatively simple two-platform affair, but with buildings and canopies on both sides. Newark was a very prosperous town, and its originating goods traffic included coal, boilers, ball-bearings, malt, plaster, clothing, sand, gravel, agricultural machinery and glue, waste leather being an inward traffic in connection with the last-named. The train service was mostly provided by fast or semi-fast workings, the former usually being King's Cross to Leeds services. With the closure to passengers of the smaller stations to the north such as Crow Park, Tuxford and Dukeries Junction (6 October 1958, 4 July 1955 and 6 March 1950 respectively) the stopping trains were progressively whittled away, there never having been a generous service. In summer 1946 Crow Park and Tuxford saw two up trains each weekday, whilst Dukeries Junction was served by only one; in the other direction there was a single all-stations Grantham to Doncaster train serving all three. In winter 1955-6, when only Crow Park remained, it had the ridiculous situation of having only one train on weekdays, the 5.52pm to Newark and Grantham, with none at all in the down direction. However, it was possible to get back there by waiting until Sunday, when the 2.40pm from Grantham (3.1pm at Newark) called at 3.12pm. No doubt a good case was made for low usage by passengers!

Muskham troughs were just under two miles beyond Newark station; special instructions required that down express freight trains not able to get a clear run past Trent box had to be stopped at Newark for water. The troughs themselves had a speed limit of 60mph, which was about the best for taking water: less and not enough could be scooped up, and more would shower everything – especially anyone rash enough to have a window open in the front coaches of the train.

There was another flat crossing at Retford, this time with the Great Central line between Sheffield and Gainsborough. It was possible for all trains to call at the main line station by means of the connecting curves between Thrumpton Crossing West junction (GC) and Retford South, and Retford North and Whiskerhill Junction (GC). The Great Central station (Thrumpton) had closed as long ago as 1859, although it remained open for goods until 1970; the Great Northern's Babworth (renamed Retford Goods in 1924), about half a mile to the north of the main station, also survived for freight until 1966.

The line north of Retford was again easy, with three miles of level track around Barnby Moor; there was then a gentle fall through Ranskill to Scrooby, where there were more troughs just on the down side of the former station, which had closed in 1931. Also at Scrooby was the junction for the Harworth Colliery branch, a single line worked on the 'one engine in steam' principle with Harworth Colliery box; a further staff was used between the colliery box and the colliery itself. There was also access from the South Yorkshire Joint line. At Bawtry, about two miles further, there was another goods-only branch to Misson, this time on the up side, also worked by train staff, with Oates siding and the Yorkshire Amalgamated Products siding having ground frames released by an Annett's key on the train staff. Bawtry loaded very large tonnages of sand and gravel – one of the largest on the LNER. There was also a water softening plant on the down side,

where old tenders were stabled for the purposes of 'sludging', together with stores wagons.

Almost at the limit of the Great Northern's main line, Rossington marked the approach to Doncaster. Loversall Carr junction gave access to the Rossington Colliery branch, and there was the maze of junctions connecting the various yards, the GN&GE joint line from Lincoln, the South Yorkshire Joint and the Great Central. The numbers of relief and goods lines multiplied on the approach to Doncaster, with some boxes signalling only in one direction, or one group of lines: Potteric Carr did not signal the down main; Decoy No 1 Down only the down lines, and Decoy No 2 the up lines and down transfer line only.

Much has been written and said about Doncaster, its station and its works – 'The Plant'. It may have marked almost the limit of the Great Northern on the main line, but its tentacles stretched much further east and west – out to Mablethorpe on the Lincolnshire coast, Bradford and Keighley. Doncaster, a major hub of the system, was rebuilt in 1936 to remedy operating bottlenecks, particularly on the up side. The result was a station of two island platforms with new buildings on the up platform in a somewhat 'art deco' style ; a tiled subway replaced the original footbridge. At the south end the works footbridge would see quite a stampede at the end of the day's shift! Doncaster was the focus for very many services: those to Hull via the North Eastern, Cleethorpes and Grimsby via the Great Central, Leeds via the GN&GC Joint, Harrogate via Knottingley, Lincoln and March via the GN&GE line (the Great Eastern had once run from Liverpool Street to York via this route) and many other branches and secondary lines.

The North Eastern Railway met the Great Northern at Shaftholme Junction, just north of Doncaster, and spread its net over a wide area. The main line was very easily graded, there being nearly eight miles of level track between Arksey and Balne, with a few gentle undulations otherwise. At Selby the line crossed the River Ouse by means of a swing bridge built in 1891, and thought in 1960 to be the busiest on British Railways. It was a focal point for East Coast main line services and the routes to Market Weighton, Hull and Leeds, but its traffic is much reduced since the main line was closed to the north because of mining subsidence. The Ouse is tidal at Selby, and in the 1950s and 60s was used by a large number of barges and sea-going vessels serving the riverside depots of Spillers and British Oil & Cake Mills. The barges were able to pass the bridge whilst it was closed, but the larger vessels required it to be swung up to six times a day.

The bridge itself was worked from a cabin astride the 130ft swinging span, whilst rail traffic was controlled by a signalbox on the south side of the river. This gave problems for many years because the pointwork on the north side could not be controlled from this cabin, and as a consequence the fast and slow down lines were interlaced across the bridge, causing much wear and difficult maintenance. In 1960 the need to renew timbers on the bridge with thicker material necessitated the raising of the control cabin to retain the necessary clearances (in fact it was raised by some 3ft more than this since they had been extremely tight). The opportunity was also taken to renew the track and signalling using remote control methods, and the down lines were relaid as a single track over the bridge. The work took place in two phases, the first involving raising the cabin in a 30hr rail occupation, followed by a 4-day closure to river traffic whilst the drive arrangements were altered. In the second stage a further 24hr rail occupation saw the track relaid and the new pointwork and signalling brought into use. A neap tide period was chosen for the former, since low water levels prevented many ships coming up the river.

The main line continued through Riccall, Escrick and Naburn, where there was another swing bridge, the line from Leeds trailing in at Chaloners Whin junction. All of these stations closed before Dr Beeching, Riccall being the last to go in 1958. They had enjoyed a very limited passenger service of two down and three up stopping trains between York and Doncaster or Selby.

The North Eastern's main stations reflected a unified approach involving large arched roofs and were monuments to design and elegance. York's present station opened in 1877, and although there have been some alterations, it remains substantially unchanged today. Its magnificent roof, arched and on a curve, covers the main lines and platforms, with other arches over the

bays. There were fourteen platforms; two more, Nos 15 and 16 were brought in as through platforms in 1951 with the resignalling, and their stark awnings contrast harshly with the older parts of the roof. Closure of some of the platforms took place in 1988-9 as the layout was prepared for electrification. York station was a place of great activity, where engines were once changed on the Scottish trains; heavy traffic from the Leeds direction; holidaymakers to Scarborough, trains to Harrogate and branches to Whitby via Pickering and Hull via Market Weighton all contributed. The situation of the station was incomparable: right by the city wall, with the covered portico leading into the booking hall, which had its NER map made from glazed wall tiles, which were a feature of so many of the company's stations.

York station was one of the largest on the North Eastern's system, being surpassed only by Newcastle, with 15 platforms. Bays at the north end were used for Scarborough trains starting at York, and also for Hull and Whitby services, the latter via Malton and Pickering, and the former via Market Weighton, both closed by BR in 1965. Platforms 12 and 13, also north end bays, were used for Harrogate and Pickering trains. Incidentally, in 1957 a cheap day return to Malton cost just 3s (15p) from York, and from Malton all the way to Whitby 6s 6d (32 ½p). The south end bays (in practice, platforms 2 and 3) could be used by any southbound train. Until the advent of the LNER, York was a crucial operational point as the location for engine changes between the North Eastern and Great Northern; afterwards as the use of Gresley's Pacifics increased they became able to work right through between London and Newcastle or Edinburgh. Crew changes still took place at York, although even this was reduced by the building of the corridor tenders for the non-stop Anglo-Scottish expresses.

Before the war York station had been controlled by four manual signalboxes (Locomotive Yard, with 295 levers in one row,

Below:
Sandy, 44 miles from King's Cross, was served by both the East Coast main line and the former LNWR route between Bletchley and Cambridge. In August 1960 Class A1 No 60119 *Patrick Stirling* runs through platform 2 with an up parcels working.
John C. Baker

Platform, Waterworks and Leeman Road), all swept away – together with Chaloners Whin, Clifton and South Points – in 1951 when the new powerbox was opened. The scheme had been inaugurated by the LNER before the war, and was then suspended, being resumed in 1946. Colour lights now extended all the way from Naburn to Darlington, with some similar installations on other approach lines. AC track circuits were installed, replacing the old DC ones, and power operation of pointwork introduced. After closure of the Locomotive Yard box it was demolished, and new pointwork laid over it to platforms 15 and 16, which were then brought into use as through platforms. With the new work 33.75 track miles and 317 track circuits came under the new box, this representing 18 miles of running lines and 5.5 miles of loop, reception and platform lines. The remainder were automatically-signalled sections linking with Copmanthorpe, Naburn Swing Bridge, Burton Lane and Skelton, which became the new fringe boxes to the west, south-east and north respectively. The new signals (74 controlled from the new box) were either three- or four-aspect colour lights, many also carrying subsidiaries below them, and others having junction or route indicators, either of the 'lunar lights' or theatre-type depending on speed of divergence; there were 154 shunting signals. Point operation largely retained the North Eastern electro-pneumatic system,

which was felt to be cheaper on maintenance and to operate quicker than all-electric types.

The new signalbox was built over parts of platforms 13 and 14, and was over 200ft long and 40ft wide, with an office for the assistant stationmasters and a 'silence cabinet' for the station announcer. Messing facilities were also provided for signalmen and maintenance staff. The illuminated panel was designed to be operated by four men, each with a section of the console, and directed by a traffic controller. A back-up generator was provided in the case of mains power failure. The scheme cost more than £500,000, but was estimated to have savings (1951 prices) of £19,680 annually in signalmen's wage costs, only 27 men being needed as against the 70 previously in the old boxes. The main contractors were the Westinghouse Brake & Signal Co Ltd, with telephones and train describers coming from Standard Telephones and Cables.

The line onwards to Darlington dated from 1841, and with the exceptions of Pilmoor and Eryholme, the stations on this section across the Vale of York also originated then. Between York and Northallerton the intermediate stations were Beningbrough, Tollerton, Alne (junction for the Easingwold railway), Raskelf, Pilmoor (junction for the line to Harrogate, and also to Gilling, Pickering and Driffield), Sessay, Thirsk and Otterington. With the obvious exception of Thirsk, their passenger service was limited; in winter 1957-8 it amounted to one train each way – the 6.40am York to Edinburgh called at all stations except Croft Spa to Darlington, and the 6.27am Darlington to Doncaster called at all stations to York except Otterington, which did get a call from the 5.15pm Northallerton-Leeds. Alne also had another up

Above:
On the other side of the station, Class K3 No 61849 passes Sandy with a parcels train from Bletchley to Cambridge, again in August 1960. The fireman prepares to exchange the train staff, although two young spotters show little interest. The station gardens provide a wonderful backdrop.
John C. Baker

evening train at 8.23pm, as well as a down at 8.54am. In common with many other rural stations their main traffic had been agricultural, especially potatoes; Tollerton loaded round timber. There was much activity from local airfields in the Second World War, and many of the stations handled petrol and other supplies. All except Tollerton closed in 1958 – it went in 1965, although Thirsk, of course, remains open.

On the main line, much widening took place between York and Northallerton, and this also involved the rebuilding of stations in some places, though in others it was avoided. At Northallerton there were already avoiding lines, but especially between the wars the LNER took the opportunity to do the work with government funding. Beningbrough and Otterington were completely rebuilt in 1933, as was the down side at Alne, where the bay for the Easingwold Light Railway was a feature of the up side. This lost its passenger service in November 1948, but goods survived another nine years. By 1957 the construction of an up slow line between Pilmoor and Alne was the only work needed to complete the provision of four tracks all the way from York (Skelton) to Northallerton. The 2.5-mile Easingwold line finally closed at the end of December.

The layout at Northallerton was complex. The line from Ripon and Harrogate trailed in on the down side at the south end of the station, whilst to the north a triangular junction gave access to the Hawes branch westwards through Wensleydale. Additionally the line to Stockton and Middlesbrough via Eaglescliffe diverged north-eastwards to the north of the station, and this could also be reached by the avoiding lines which joined the main line to the south and burrowed under them to the north. Best to look at a track plan to make sense of it!

Northwards from Northallerton, water troughs were installed in the middle of the 3.5-mile level stretch to Danby Wiske, with Cowton, Eryholme and Croft Spa stations before reaching Darlington; Eryholme was the junction for the Richmond branch, a busy line with up to 13 trains each way daily. Eryholme handled only goods for many years, losing its passenger service in 1911, surviving for freight until 1964.

Darlington, as well as being one of the original homes of railways in Britain, had an interesting railway system. It was the focus for a number of lines, the one from Stockton being suffixed North Road. Until 1887 trains from Stockton had run via Fighting Cocks to North Road, and could not easily call at the main line station, Bank Top. In that year a new line via Dinsdale was opened which obviated the problem, leaving Fighting Cocks as a goods-only station; it meant that east-west trains from Saltburn and the coast to Barnard Castle and Tebay could now connect with main line services. Trains could also go via Bishop Auckland to the Weardale line for Stanhope and Wearhead, which carried very heavy traffic from the many quarries, and also to Consett and even Durham via Hunwick and Willington. Much of the area was important for the heavy mineral traffic that had been the lifeblood of the North Eastern, and this particular line served Brandon Colliery and saw some regular through services, at least in the 1950s, from Middleton-in-Teesdale to Sunderland – from the rural idyll at one end to the heavy industrial heartland at the other. Whilst a few colliery lines still exist, the Weardale branch hangs on by the skin of its teeth hoping for preservation, its last regular passenger trains having run on Saturday 27 June 1953; Consett, Barnard Castle and Stainmore are long gone, and Bishop Auckland is the sole destination for passenger services to the west of Darlington.

Bank Top station is set on a loop to the west of the main line itself. The station is built as an island with bays set at each end, and a splendid building and overall roof spanning it all. For many years one of its features was Stockton & Darlington Railway locomotive No 1 on its display stand, which had been authorised by the NER as long ago as 1891, later to be joined by S&DR *Derwent*, but they were removed in 1975. Another relic of these very earliest days was for many years the level rail crossing of the original Stockton & Darlington line by the ECML about a mile north of Bank Top station at the junction with the Bishop Auckland line, although the North Eastern's rule book was quite explicit that coal trains on the former were always to give way to passenger trains on the latter.

The main line swept onwards from Darlington, being easily graded with some level sections. Falling from Bradbury through Ferryhill, there was a complex series of junctions, with a line once going to Hartlepool, the goods-only Coxhoe branch (closed in 1966) and the 'old main line' to Gateshead and Newcastle via Fencehouses, Pelaw and Brockley Whins. Later the present main line was built from Tursdale junction, north of Ferryhill, to Relly Mill south of Durham. Whilst most express trains ran via the latter route the old line continued to see some such traffic, including diversions. Relly Mill was actually one of the highest points on the line, and having passed Durham it continued to fall, through Chester-le-Street almost to Low Fell, only about three miles from Newcastle.

Newcastle Central was the largest and busiest of the North Eastern's stations, and in some respects resembled York. On the north bank of the River Tyne, it was orientated on a curve on an east-west axis, though its major services ran from north to south. It was also the focus for the North Eastern's only real suburban service, most of what remains now being incorporated into the Tyne & Wear Metro. Designed originally by John Dobson, the station was first opened in 1850 and featured a soaring main arched roof, flanked by three smaller arches, although the colonnade and portico were not provided until 1863. Local trains to the coast used bay platforms at the east end of the station on the north side, and this meant that trains from the lines over the High Level bridge conflicted with those from the coast via Manors at the much-photographed 'largest railway crossing in the world', with its myriad cast manganese steel diamonds. Trains to Carlisle used bays at the west end, but for a station of its importance, it is perhaps surprising that Newcastle had only three through platforms. It saw electric trains at a very early date, of course, since the North Eastern had first electrified some of its services on Tyneside in 1904 on the 600V third-rail system, in response to intense competition from trams. Trains ran on a circular route from Newcastle Central via Tynemouth and Whitley Bay, with the South Shields service introduced in 1938 ; both survived well into British Railways days.

Until the King Edward bridge was constructed in 1906 ECML trains had to reverse at Newcastle; since then they have been able to arrive via any route and depart via any route. The 'Flying Scotsman' did not run through Newcastle without stopping until 1928, but this facility has certainly been used in British Railways days by this and other named trains. In 1959 extensive resignalling was undertaken in the area. Where before there had been five electro-pneumatic boxes at Central and the approaches from Gateshead, boasting some 960 levers between them (Newcastle East and West boxes respectively had 283 and 211 levers) four of the five were replaced by a route-relay box at the centre of the station. This allowed better train control and greater economy of working.

To the north of Newcastle the ECML was more of a switchback, generally rising to Cramlington, and then falling towards Alnmouth, although the gradients were by no means constant or consistent. Acklington was a former North Eastern station about six miles south of Alnmouth. In the 1950s it still retained its own stationmaster, whose duties also involved the supervision of Chevington, the next station to the south. The signalbox there was unusual in that it also controlled Amble Junction by means of power-operated points, using a hand generator. The station was kept busy by the considerable level of RAF personnel travelling to and from the nearby base, where the runways were so close to the main line that a trip-wire was connected to emergency signals for the protection of trains. The volume of personnel going on leave sometimes necessitated making special arrangements. The everyday train service was provided by semi-fasts between Newcastle and Edinburgh, and stoppers between Newcastle and Alnwick or Berwick. Seven trains called in the down direction on winter weekdays in 1957-8, with an extra on Friday and Saturday. It was also a centre for anglers fishing the River Coquet for salmon and trout. Considerable coal traffic was handled, as well as pigeons in season, and a weekly cattle market also contributed. The staff still found time to enter the station gardens competition, winning a first-class certificate in 1955 and a special class, worth £8, in 1960.

Between Acklington and the next station to the north, Warkworth, the main line crossed the River Coquet by means of a viaduct, a structure of nine 50ft arch spans and two 12ft approach spans, which had to be strengthened in the early 1950s. Serious deterioration had been evident for some time, with remedial attention given as long ago as 1925. The work consisted firstly of providing tie-bars between all piers to reduce the spread under load, the bars being made of old rail and placed immediately below springing level, securely bolted through the piers. Following this reinforced concrete arches were constructed under the brickwork of each span, using steel-frame centring, both to limit deformation and to remove the need to cut out and replace the defective brickwork forming the arches. Deflection tests carried out in July 1953 showed that the desired effect had been achieved.

Northwards again, Alnmouth was the junction for the 3-mile Alnwick branch, still the recipient of through trains from Newcastle in 1958. Local stations enjoyed a reasonable service of stopping trains throughout the 1950s; Chathill had ceased to be a junction in 1951 when the North Sunderland light railway to Seahouses closed. There were water troughs just to the south of Lucker station which had closed to passengers in 1953. Tweedmouth, 65.25 miles from Newcastle, was the junction for Coldstream, Kelso and St Boswells, the branch losing most of its local stations in the 1950s, and by 1958 it saw only two trains each way daily from Berwick. From the Royal Border Bridge the ECML became part of the Scottish Region, although still worked as an entity as it always had been, with important allocations of Pacifics to Haymarket. Heavy investment in the 1980s has seen the East Coast main line eclipse the West Coast route, with electrification and the new '225' trains worthy successors to Gresley's streamliners.

CHAPTER 2 Locomotives of the East Coast Main Line

Throughout its existence the East Coast main line had demanded the highest standards of locomotive engineering, driving and maintenance, and the insistent competition with the West Coast had pushed it on to ever-greater heights. Sir Nigel Gresley had had enormous influence, from his time with the Great Northern, through his years with the LNER until his death in April 1941. He was replaced as Chief Mechanical Engineer by Edward Thompson, who retired in June 1946, and who had instituted many changes to Gresley's locomotives, much to the wrath of many enthusiasts. Arthur H. Peppercorn became the last CME of the LNER, and in his relatively short tenure of the post left his mark on many of the designs. He retired at the end of 1949, with J. F. Harrison taking up the post of Mechanical & Electrical Engineer.

In 1950 the principal express trains were in the hands of the ex-LNER Pacifics, which were in the process of being repainted into British Railways colours. The main depots were at King's Cross, Gateshead and Edinburgh, with others at Grantham, Peterborough and York. New locomotives were still being built

to LNER designs, of course, and in January 1950 five new Class A1 Pacifics were at work (Nos 60153-7), being notable for their roller bearing axleboxes. Of these Nos 60156/7 went to King's Cross, and Nos 60154/5 to Gateshead for working the Tyne-Tees Pullman service, and covered over 2,400 miles per week in so doing. Another particularly exacting duty involved the Night Scotsman (10.15pm from King's Cross) which was scheduled to run non-stop to Newcastle; the advanced portion of the up train was also similarly scheduled, leaving Edinburgh at 9.40pm.

The locomotives themselves were not infrequently transferred between sheds, with various modifications and improvements made from time to time. In February 1950, for example, 'A2s' No 60501 Cock o' the North, No 60502 Earl Marischal and No 60503 Lord President went from Scotland to York, all of

Below:
Peterborough North sees 'A3' No 60099 Call Boy easing under the bridge with a down express in July 1961.
John C. Baker

them also being in the process of being painted in the new dark green livery with the BR totem. At the same time Nos 60158-62 were being allocated new to King's Cross and Edinburgh, whilst there was a proposal to rebuild No 60113 *Great Northern*, Gresley's original Pacific, as an 'A1'. In March it had been repainted into BR blue livery and transferred to King's Cross as the only representative of Class A1/1. 'A3' Pacific No 60103 *Flying Scotsman* was also now in blue, and a member of this class often worked the 7.55am up from Newcastle, due at King's Cross at 1.35pm and returning at 5.35pm. In June there was a major reallocation of the Pacifics, with new 'A1s' going to Copley Hill (Leeds). Half of the 34 streamlined 'A4s' were now at King's Cross, with eight at Newcastle, seven at Edinburgh and two at Grantham.

The engines certainly earnt their keep. Grantham 'A4' No 60030 *Golden Fleece* covered 30,000 miles between November 1949 and Easter 1950. In a fortnight it typically worked seven trips to King's Cross and back, and six to Newcastle and

back, making a total of 3,433 miles. 'A4' No 60022 Mallard was a regular on the 'Tyne Tees Pullman', working down one evening and back up the next. On alternate days it also worked the 2.34am papers from King's Cross to Grantham, returning to King's Cross in time to take the 4.45am to Newcastle. Weekends saw the locomotive working from King's Cross to Newcastle or Grantham, covering 8,800 miles in four weeks. 'A4' No 60029 *Woodcock* followed *Mallard* on these rosters.

The winter 1951-2 timetable saw the 'Capitals Limited', non-stop between King's Cross and Edinburgh worked by 'A4s' No 60017 *Silver Fox* and No 60033 *Seagull*, with No 60011 *Dominion of India* and No 60024 *Kingfisher* the Scottish engines. The up 'Scotsman' was reported as being worked on several occasions between Grantham and King's Cross by Class V2 2-6-2s – and gaining up to seven minutes! In fact these fine engines had a nominal tractive effort slightly higher than an 'A3', although their driving wheel diameter, at 6ft 2in was 6in smaller. A less usual working was that of 'A4' No 60032 *Gannet*, which hauled the King's Cross steam crane to Doncaster, both being due for the works.

Other services were handled by some of the less glamorous engines, such as Edward Thompson's highly-successful 4-6-0 'B1s', first introduced in 1942. May 1950 saw the introduction of Immingham-based members of the class on the Cleethorpes buffet car express, which ran to King's Cross via Louth, Boston and Spalding, and which was the first regular working of Immingham locomotives into London. 'Green Arrows', otherwise known as 'V2s' were often pressed into passenger service at times such as Easter weekend, when large numbers of extra third class trains would be run to ease congestion, although they also found regular passenger use on services such as the Cambridge buffet car expresses, when they replaced 'B1s'.

Near the end of 1950 the last of H. A. Ivatt's Great Northern Atlantics, No 62822 – built in 1905 – made its farewell trip from King's Cross to Doncaster, where it was taken out of service.

Left:

A busy scene at High Dyke loop on 8 August 1962 as 'V2' No 60871 lifts the York-King's Cross train up the bank towards Stoke tunnel. Meanwhile 'WD' No 90223 blows off as it waits in the loop.

J. M. Rayner

Below left:

Class O2 2-8-0 No 63931 ambles past Skillington Road junction with a brake van on 16 April 1963. The goods-only branch served mines at Colsterworth, Stainby, Sproxton and Cringle.

Ian Allan Library

Though they only just made it into the British Railways era, these fine engines had been stalwarts of the ECML for many years. The first, massive for its time, had appeared as long ago as 1898, later being given the name *Henry Oakley* after the General Manager of the company. Ten similar engines were built in 1900, and they worked on the main line for a number of years. *Henry Oakley* was preserved by the LNER and is now part of the National Collection. In 1902 Ivatt brought out a further type of Atlantic, this time with a much larger boiler (5ft 6in diameter instead of 4ft 8in), and this class multiplied to a total of 83 by 1908, with a further 10 superheated members being added in 1910. A number of modifications were made over the years, all of them becoming superheated and many receiving piston valves. They became renowned for their work on the King's Cross-Leeds Pullmans, being replaced by Gresley's Pacifics as they became available. With the exception of No 3292 in 1927 withdrawal did not start until 1943, No 62822 being the last survivor.

December 1950 saw further allocations of 'A3s' to Grantham, which had now acquired 12 of the class. More 'A1s' were being fitted with double chimneys including the newly-named No 60157 *Great Eastern*, recently out-shopped in green livery. It had been decided to name 'A1' Pacifics Nos 60147 and 60156

North Eastern and *Great Central* respectively, although neither had so far been executed. (No 60147 was finally named in May 1952, and No 60156 in September, being out-shopped in dark green at the same time). However, Darlington works was now building LMR 2-6-0s, although five more B1s were delivered (4 going to Peterborough and 1 to Doncaster), with six more awaited to complete the class total of 410.

Wednesday 16 October 1957 marked the end of an era at Doncaster works, when BR Standard Class 4 No 76114 was completed and ready for traffic: the last steam locomotive to be built at 'The Plant'. It had seen the birth of many famous engines, from Great Northern 0-4-2 No 18, the first to be built there in 1867, through the Stirling 8ft 'Singles', the Ivatt Atlantics and the Gresley, Thompson and Peppercorn Pacifics. Ironically, the rolling-out of No 76114 coincided with the commencement of a programme of building 350hp diesel-electric shunters. The association with steam was not to be severed immediately, since it was envisaged that the programme of some 700 classified locomotive repairs annually would continue for some time. By 1960 diesels were starting to appear on the King's Cross to Newcastle trains, although they were often replaced by 'A3s' or 'A4s'. Even so, withdrawals were occurring with increasing frequency, though others were still being put through the works. At the start of December 1959 there were still 19 'A4s' and 13 'A3s' at King's Cross, but by 1962 'Deltics' were infiltrating services, and some of the Pacifics ended their days on the main lines in eastern Scotland with a wonderful swansong on the line to Aberdeen.

Below:

Grantham North box sees Class L1 No 67796 heading the 1.7pm local to Derby Friargate on 4 August 1962, whilst 'A2' No 60520 *Owen Tudor* pulls away on the down main with the 1.8pm slow to Doncaster.

J. M. Rayner

Left:

In May 1961 Class J6 No 64245, with a brake van in tow, comes off the Great Central line on to the Great Northern at Retford.
John C. Baker

Below:

A Robinson 'J11', No 64324, ambles through Retford with a mineral train in August 1962.
J. Hollingworth

Right:

Class A1 No 60139 *Sea Eagle* passes through Doncaster in April 1960 with an up express, while a Class 114 DMU waits with a local service to Sheffield.
John C. Baker

Below right:

Class O2 No 63943 draws up to the water column at Doncaster with a down coal train in April 1961. The back of the train stretches under the footbridge connecting the works and station.
John C. Baker

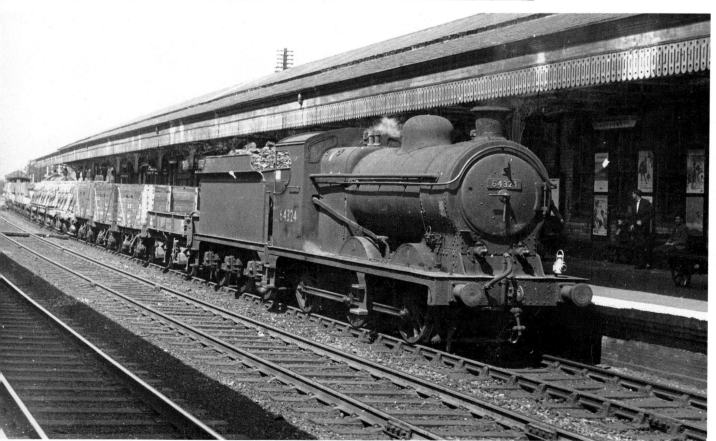

Right:
Class V3 No 67638, of Neville Hill (Leeds) shed, lurks in a siding at Doncaster in April 1960.
John C. Baker

Below right:
'A2/2' No 60502 *Earl Marischal* heads a Newcastle-King's Cross train through Selby on Saturday 6 August 1960. The new signalling is now by colour-lights, following the extensive bridge work earlier in the year.
B. Webb

Below:
'J6' No 64264 comes off Selby swing bridge and past the North box with an express goods on 3 September 1954. The fine North Eastern bracket signal still sports slotted posts, while everybody knows that Virol is 'The Food for Health'.
R. S. Potts

CHAPTER 3
East Coast Main Line Services

The East Coast main line emerged from the war years with services recognisable by comparison with the late 1930s. The main daytime trains still ran to Hull, Leeds, York, Newcastle and Edinburgh, whilst sleepers ran every night to Edinburgh and Aberdeen in the form of the 'Night Scotsman' and 'Aberdonian', as well as a Fridays-only train to Fort William, which returned on Monday afternoon. A host of fast, semi-fast and stopping services plied the route, although the wayside stations might only see two or three trains in each direction.

1948 was not a good year for ECML services. The government had imposed mileage restrictions resulting from the fuel shortage due to the severe weather in February and March 1947, and thousands of trains were cut out. On 11-12 August severe storms in the north of England and the Scottish borders caused widespread flooding, with many streams and rivers bursting their banks and damaging railway tracks and embankments. Seven bridges were washed out between Grantshouse and Reston, just north of Berwick, and an embankment destroyed by the Pease Burn between Grantshouse and Cockburnspath. The main line was blocked in 11 places between Newcastle and Berwick, but was reopened as far as the latter on 14 August, temporary bridges having been installed to release some of the floodwater.

The 'Flying Scotsman' had left King's Cross at 10.00am as usual on 12 August and after reaching Newcastle had to be diverted via Carlisle and Carstairs, reaching Edinburgh at 3.51am, some ten hours late. Other diversions were arranged, for example southbound via St Boswells, Kelso and Tweedmouth, which was only 5.5 miles longer than via the main line, but over single track branch lines. Temporary timetables were instituted, and the overall delays reduced to between 60 and 90 minutes. The first freight train was able to pass over the restored main line on Monday 25 October, and passenger services restarted on 1 November, diversions having been in place in the meantime. The final restrictions were removed from 5 June 1950 when the new summer timetable was introduced, all the bridges and embankments having finally been replaced.

Apart from all this, track deterioration was still proving to be a problem as the arrears of maintenance from the war were caught up. By the summer timetables of 1949 many of the cuts imposed

Below:
North of Selby 'A4' No 60033 Seagull speeds over a level crossing near Riccall with the up 'Flying Scotsman' in August 1960.
John C. Baker

Above:

In April 1959 York station sees the departure of Class A2 No 60518 *Tehran* with an up express.
John C. Baker

earlier had been restored, and the 'Tyne-Tees Pullman' had returned. A new non-stop train, the 'Capitals Limited' between King's Cross and Edinburgh had been introduced, together with faster services between King's Cross and Leeds with the 'White Rose' and 'West Riding'. Autumn 1949 saw the first postwar 60mph schedule on the North Eastern Region. Even so, there were still some gaps in the summer 1950 timetables by comparison with winter of 1947-8, although there were more services on the ECML than in 1939. Among the named trains these additions included the 'Northumbrian' (King's Cross to Newcastle, sometimes going through to the Tyne Commission Quay) and the 'West Riding'. However, most of the semi-fast trains north of Grantham had gone, and there was a general worsening in the provision of through coaches largely brought about by shortages of rolling stock. Other cuts were also beginning to appear, and all through fares for the Lancashire, Derbyshire and East Coast (LD&EC) line were withdrawn. On 6 March 1950 Dukeries Junction closed, both the main line and LD&EC platforms, although the route did not actually close until some years after.

The East Coast main line was the undoubted star of the Eastern and North Eastern Regions as far as train performance was concerned. In the summer of 1955 108 miles were scheduled to be covered at a speed in excess of 66mph, which was a single run. 258 miles (three runs) were covered at over 64mph, 424 miles (nine runs) at over 62mph and 1972 miles (21 runs) at over 60mph. All but one of these was on the ECML, the sole exception being the 4.46pm from Ipswich to Norwich.

The most famous express train of all was, of course, the 'Flying Scotsman'. Its genesis was in 1862 when the 'Special Scotch Express' first ran, leaving King's Cross at 10.00am, with the corresponding up working from Edinburgh at the same time. The train then took some 10.5hr for its journey over a route which differed in detail from that in its centenary year, 1962. Having progressed from haulage by Stirling Singles and Ivatt Atlantics the

first non-stop run was made on 1 May 1928, appropriately behind Gresley's 'A3' No 4472 *Flying Scotsman*. In 1935 the streamlined 'A4' Pacifics took over regular working, with steam not being superseded until 1958 when Type 4 diesel-electric No D207 made the first run with this type of traction. By the time of its centenary the 3,300hp 'Deltics' had taken over, bringing the timings down to six hours. Always a prestige working, the train enjoyed the most up-to-date rolling stock, and by the 1950s it was composed of standard BR Mark 1 steel stock, retaining one of its original features in that it was still a two-class supplement-free service.

In the 1946 summer timetable, the 'Scotsman', leaving King's Cross at its time-honoured hour of 10.00am called at Peterborough – where it paused for a full eight minutes – and York, Newcastle and Berwick, arriving in Edinburgh at 6.18pm. There were scheduled relief trains from King's Cross at 9.30 and 9.45am, calling at Grantham and not Peterborough, and both missing Berwick, although only the 'Scotsman' carried a restaurant car.

Above right:

'V2' No 60868 heads northwards with a freight at Poppleton, on the York-Harrogate line.
Eric Treacy

Right:

On the Leeds Northern, Sinderby was a small wayside station between Melmerby and Northallerton. Here, 'V2' No 60947 heads a Harrogate-Leeds train on 16 August 1960. Sinderby lost its passenger services at the start of 1962.
R. E. James-Robertson

This, of course, represented a considerable improvement over the war years, when the train had taken 8.25 hours and had no refreshment service at all, although restaurant cars still ran to Leeds and Hull, and when it also called at Doncaster. Another minor point of note was that the LNER, in spite of owning and operating the ECML throughout, split the public timetables into three sections (table 1 from King's Cross to York, 103 from York to Newcastle and 157 from Newcastle to Edinburgh) which were all printed in the same book, although summaries were also provided at the front. When British Railways took over the line was split between three regions, and it was necessary to consult at least two timetable books for the three sections, the North Eastern publishing both the parts north and south of Newcastle.

In winter 1951-2 the stop at Peterborough had been replaced with one at Grantham, but York and Berwick had been omitted, Newcastle being the only other stop: through coaches were left there for the Tyne Commission Quay on Wednesdays and Saturdays. Edinburgh was reached in 7hr 50min. By the winter of 1955-6 the timing was down to 7 hours 30 minutes, calling only at Grantham and Newcastle, with the up train conveying through coaches from Aberdeen and Dundee (Tay Bridge). The formation included a restaurant car, buffet lounge car and Ladies Retiring Rooms with attendants. The third class single fare was 61s 8d (£3.08). Summer 1958 saw Newcastle as the only intermediate stop, and the overall time down to 6hr 58min, although in winter it crept back to 7hr 2min. The 'Elizabethan' was doing the journey non-stop in summer, leaving King's Cross at 9.30am and taking only 6hr 35min; the fare had risen to 65s 6d (£3.28). The following summer saw the same timings on weekdays, and also the return of the 'Elizabethan', but it was not long before the diesels arrived. By 1962 the 'Deltics' had slashed the time to just 6hr, again with one stop at Newcastle, and with through coaches serving Aberdeen in both directions. With the coming of the InterCity 125s, coupled with much heavy engineering work over a number of years (rebuilding of Peterborough station, elimination of Offord curves, new lines around Selby and Penmanshiel tunnel to name but a few) the time was brought down to around 4hr 8min – but that is quite another story.

Among all this glory one unsung group of people deserves a mention – the carriage cleaners, whose work probably had more immediate impact on the passengers than anyone else's. Wood Green Carriage Depot dealt with the complete range of trains – main line, outer suburban, parcels and even sleeping and dining cars for the King's Cross Great Northern district. With 82 sidings able to accommodate 920 coaches, the staff dealt with between 1,580 and 2,500 trains weekly, involving up to 5,000 coaches in the summer; this included 3,500 sleeping berths in winter and 7,500 in summer. Around 100 women did the work, involving general cleaning, cleaning of sleeping cars and making beds, six women being employed all year round on the latter, with an extra two in summer. Apart from the general work they also gave the stock a periodic 'spring clean', involving the washing down of walls and ceilings and the polishing of compartments and corridors – the unsung heroines of the ECML.

Below:
Under gathering storm clouds 'A2' No 60526 *Sugar Palm* at the head of the 'Queen of Scots' Pullman overtakes 'B1' No 61254 near Northallerton.
Eric Treacy

Left:
At Wiske Moor troughs Class A1 No 60131 *Osprey* takes water whilst heading the down 'Flying Scotsman' in August 1951.
Locomotive Publishing Co 24679

Below left:
On Saturday 23 July 1960 the 12.7pm Darlington-Bishop Auckland-Newcastle train comes off the Bishop Auckland line and crosses the viaduct at Relly Mill, with 'B1' No 61032 *Stembok* in charge.
I. S. Carr

Below:
A special train conveying Princess Alexandra arrives at Durham station on Saturday 27 July 1963, headed by 'K1' No 62024.
I. S. Carr

Left:

On a murky August day in 1960 Class Q6 No 63408 passes Newcastle Central with a freight.

John C. Baker

Below left:

On 25 August 1960 'A2/3' Pacific No 60517 *Ocean Swell* runs into Newcastle Central over the famous diamond crossings with the up 'Queen of Scots' Pullman.

I. S. Carr

Below:

In March 1966 Class J27 No 65880 (with extended smokebox) crosses the High Level bridge at Newcastle with coal empties from Stella North power station to Sunderland.

M. Dunnett

Right:

'A4' Pacific No 60032 *Gannet* approaches Newcastle Central from Manors, with the 9.45am Edinburgh Waverley to King's Cross train on Saturday 27 August 1960.

I. S. Carr

Below right:

'A1' Pacific No 60127 crosses the Royal Border Bridge at Berwick with the down 'Queen of Scots' Pullman in August 1949. The engine was later named *Wilson Worsdell*.

Real Photos 3176

Right:

Class A3 No 60105 *Victor Wild* **coasts down towards Wakefield Westgate with a Leeds-King's Cross express.**

Kenneth Field

Below right:

A Leeds-Doncaster local train, headed by 'A4' Pacific No 60139 *Sea Eagle* **waits at Wakefield Westgate.**

Eric Treacy

Below:

'V2' No 60872 *King's Own Yorkshire Light Infantry* **emerges from the tunnel at Ardsley with a King's Cross to Leeds and Bradford express.**

Kenneth Field

CHAPTER 4
Great Northern Lines

The Great Northern Railway had been conceived as a high speed route between London and the north, and was built and laid out with this in mind. In fact, the railway's first trains ran in Lincolnshire on what became secondary lines, the first being between New Holland and Louth in April 1848. By the end of the year the East Lincolnshire line had opened through to Firsby, Boston and Peterborough, and also between Boston and Lincoln. Two years later the main line to London opened from Peterborough, but the direct route between there and Retford had to wait another year. The system was progressively extended as the company sought additional traffic, and in the end it went almost as far from east to west across the country as it did from north to south. The GNR system formed a substantial part of the LNER's Southern area, and much of it went into the Eastern Region when nationalisation came along. Parts were incorporated into the North Eastern Region, notably around Leeds and Bradford, but together with the former Great Eastern and Great Central lines it made up the operational Eastern Region.

The Great Northern did not have all that many London suburban lines. However, there were intensive workings into the capital along both the main line and Hertford loop, although the latter did not start until the 1920s. There had been the branches to the Northern Heights-Edgware, Alexandra Palace and High Barnet – but these had mostly been taken over by the Underground soon

after the war, and diverted to the Northern Line tube, having once connected with the main line at Finsbury Park. The Ally Pally branch fared less well, and after the war electrification was aborted even though work had been quite advanced, including new structural steelwork for the extra platforms at Finsbury Park. There had already been a suspension of the service in the winter of 1951-2, although it resumed in January of 1952, running at peak hours only. However, the last trains ran on 3 July 1954, although the vestiges of Eastern Region freight traffic were not withdrawn until 1956 from Muswell Hill and 1957 from Cranley Gardens. The Barnet branch had been duly electrified as part of the Northern Line extension, and it had been the intention also to electrify the branch from Finchley Church End to Edgware; in the event current reached only as far as Mill Hill East and the remainder was closed. The upshot of all this was that after 1954 the only British Railways traffic over the High Barnet branch was freight and some excursion traffic, which ran until the bridges

Below:
Class L1 No 67745 approaches Barrowby Road box, where the Nottingham line joins the East Coast main line about half a mile north of Grantham. It heads the 10.30am Derby Friargate to Grantham local on 9 August 1962.
J. M. Rayner

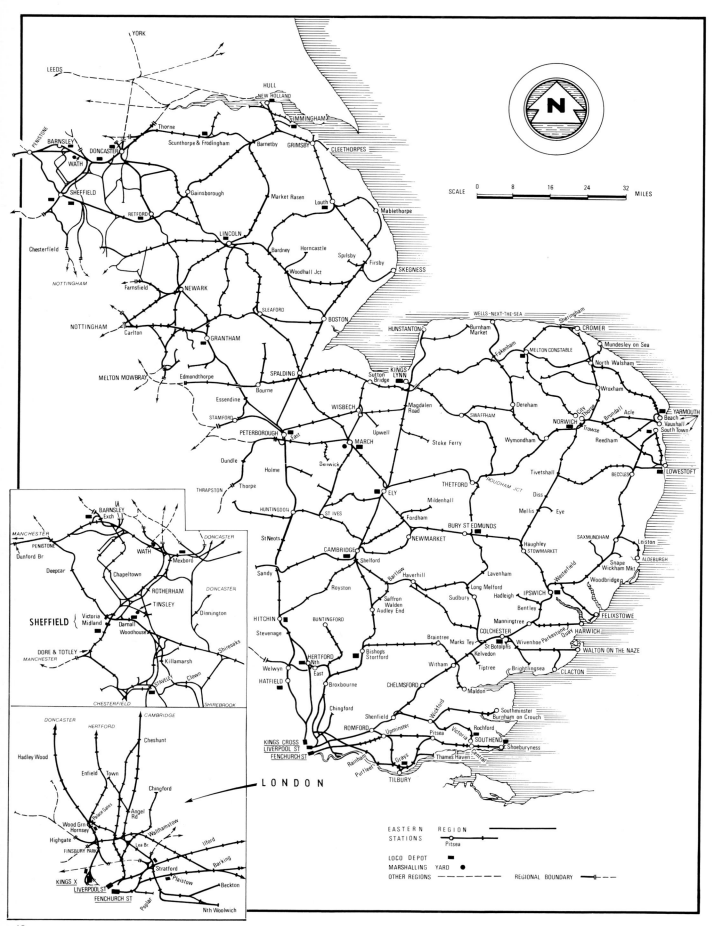

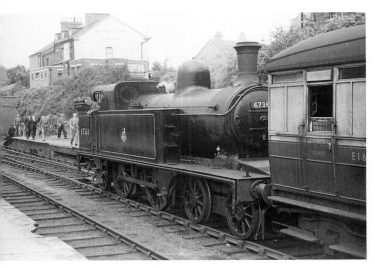

south of East Finchley allegedly became unsafe, and was withdrawn in 1964.

It is difficult to disentangle the Hertford loop from the ECML proper, and for many years it was regarded by the LNER as the relief lines, since sections of the main line were still only double track, notably from Greenwood (New Barnet) northwards, and through Welwyn North and its tunnel and viaduct. However, Hatfield, Welwyn Garden City and Hertford were connected by the old branch to Cowbridge (Hertford), which for passengers was largely made redundant by the Hertford loop, and in British Railways days had all but expired. In 1951 there was one train each way on Mondays to Fridays between St Albans and Hatfield, withdrawn from 1 October of that year. There was another branch to Dunstable from Welwyn Garden City, which enjoyed a much better service, as well it might, since the line also passed through Luton (Bute Street), Harpenden (East) and Wheathampstead, providing (in conjunction with the LNWR Dunstable-Leighton Buzzard branch) a valuable link between three main lines. Recent attempts to reopen the Luton-Dunstable section seem to have come to nothing, although the line remains in place. The line to Hertford (latterly operated in practice from Welwyn Garden City) carried five trains each way on weekdays (six on Saturdays) in the 1946 timetable, but closed in June 1951 to passengers, lingering until 1962 for goods.

The next secondary line was that from Hitchin to Cambridge, always worked by the GNR in spite of its part-ownership in pre-grouping days by the Great Eastern. It was operated with a fast through service from King's Cross – the so-called 'beer trains', although there was reasonable intermediate traffic from Baldock and Royston, and latterly Letchworth, opened in 1913. After diverging sharply from the ECML at Cambridge Junction, some 400yd north of Hitchin station, the line fell for a little before climbing steadily towards Letchworth, where there were extensive goods yards on both sides of the line, and numerous private sidings leading to various lineside factories. As late as 1962 the majority of the staff there (43 out of 58) were involved with goods traffic, which was principally paper and punch cards for computer use, minerals and general merchandise. Outwards went trailers, castings and machinery, together with horticultural traffic such as bulbs, seeds and fertilisers. At Baldock the lines passed over the Great North Road (the A1), the town later being by-passed by the A1(M). There were small goods yards here, and carriage sidings for overnight stabling. Scrap iron provided one of its largest goods traffics, and it also despatched 13,137 parcels in 1962 – 95% from the lingerie firm of Kayser Bondor. Illustrating the dedication often to be found in railway staff, Senior Porter Cecil Billings lived in a house at the end of the platform, and had spent 43 of his 47 years of railway service at the station. From the next stop, Ashwell & Morden, the line fell steadily for almost nine miles. The countryside became rather flatter after Ashwell, and there were six level crossings on the next section.

Royston was just over 44.25 miles from King's Cross, and had extensive goods yards serving a number of industrial concerns, including eight private sidings. In 1962 it was a busy and expanding station, handling 138,000 tons of merchandise. It saw two daily trainloads of petrol, and loaded huge quantities of barley for Scotland. Other sources of goods revenue included racehorses, fertilisers, pigs and mushrooms, and up to 1,000 boxes of carnations might be despatched daily. From here the line swung sharply to the left, falling towards Meldreth & Melbourn, and including 1.25 miles at 1 in 120, which had sometimes been too much for up freight trains. At Meldreth all of the facilities were on the down side; it was in the middle of fine fruit growing countryside. The line continued to fall towards Shepreth, once the limit of the Great Northern's territory, with the station being on a sharp curve to the east; it had small goods yards on both sides of the line and a level crossing to the west of the station. Outward

goods traffic here included lime, mushrooms, watercress and day-old chicks. After the former boundary at milepost 50, the line rose towards Foxton where the main Cambridge road (A10) intersected the line at a busy level crossing. Here too was a short branch to Eastwoods cement works at Barrington, whose traffic accounted for most of the 126,270 tons of freight at Foxton in 1962. Harston station, about two miles further, was the only casualty on the line, closing to passengers in 1963. Shepreth Branch Junction was approached on a very sharp curve, it being just over 55.75 miles from King's Cross, and Great Northern trains thus arrived at Cambridge over the Great Eastern main line from Liverpool Street.

The Hitchin-Cambridge line had once been signalled almost entirely with the characteristic Great Northern somersaults, many of them surviving into the 1950s, although there had been a continuous programme of replacement with upper quadrants. Stan-

Above:
On 23 February 1966 'B1' No 61302 brings a load of ore off the Denton branch on to the Grantham-Nottingham line at Belvoir and heads for Colwick Yard.
A. J. Clarke

Right:
The forlorn station at Alexandra Palace forming the terminus of the line from Highgate and Finsbury Park. It had several goes at closing, finally succumbing on 5 July 1954.
Locomotive & General 26855

dard three-position block instruments were in use on the Great Northern sections, with the Tyers two-position block on the Great Eastern parts between Shepreth Branch Junction and Cambridge. It formed a useful diversionary route for those occasions when there was a problem on the main line, and provided some of the rare opportunities to see Pacifics in Cambridge. When blockages occurred on the line into Liverpool Street trains also used the route, being diverted in the down direction via Langley Junction and the Hertford loop, thence over the connection to the Palace Gates branch at Bounds Green in order to get to the terminus. Other occasional traffic saw racegoers *en route* to Newmarket, and the Royal Train to or from Wolferton, Liverpool Street not being favoured since it was in the City of London.

Immediately after the war the timetable showed only nine stopping trains each way on the line, with others running for part of the way, and the 6.15am from Hitchin terminating at Meldreth & Melbourn. Many of the workings were third class only. By the 1951 timetable the buffet car expresses had reappeared, all stopping at Letchworth and some at Baldock and Royston as well, and taking just over 1hr 30min for the whole journey. By 1959 diesel units had been introduced on some of the stopping services, with some working only between Cambridge and Baldock. The buffet car expresses still ran, but one in the evening turned round at Royston; otherwise there were several trains from King's Cross which terminated at Baldock. By Dr Beeching's time little had changed, except that it had become almost wholly dieselised; the buffet car expresses did the journey throughout in about 1hr 25min, and he expressed no intention of altering it in his report. The only real change came much later when electrification reached Royston, when the buffet car trains were withdrawn and all services terminated there, with a shuttle onwards to Cambridge. Now that the gap has been plugged, a buffet service of sorts (using mobile trolleys) has operated again.

Further north, the Ramsey branch (or rather twig) had run out from Holme. It was not until Peterborough that the Great Northern expanded into the areas surrounding the main line, but from then on it did so effectively. The southern parts of Lincolnshire were almost its sole preserve, the East Lincs line being an important secondary route to the ports of Boston and Grimsby, as well as giving access to the resorts of Skegness, Mablethorpe and Sutton-on-Sea. Indeed, it was laid out in a manner far more suited to that of a main line than a branch. The Boston-Lincoln line was opened at the same time, closely following the course of the River Witham, but failed to serve Horncastle, to which a local company built a 7.5-mile line from Woodhall Junction. This had lost its passenger service by September 1954, remaining open for freight and worked on the one-engine-in-steam principle. Spilsby was in a similar situation, being the terminus of a short branch inland from Firsby. Much smaller than Horncastle, it lost its passenger trains soon after the outbreak of war in 1939, but again retained a goods service, and seemed to be doing quite good business when visited as late as 1958: it promptly closed at the end of the year.

The Louth-Lincoln line was another single track, with passing loops at Donington-on-Bain and Wragby. It just survived into British Railways ownership: it had two tunnels, at Withcall and South Willingham, some fierce gradients and a poor service of four passenger trains a day, down to three by 1951 which finished on 5 November of that year; the section between Louth and Donington-on-Bain closed completely from September 1956. The lines to Skegness and Mablethorpe were a different matter. The Skegness branch joined the East Lincs line at Firsby, but trains from Boston could run direct and avoid the junction station by means of a south curve, which obviated reversal. The branch had initially been built as far as Wainfleet, where the station does not seem to have been planned as a through one: the onward continuation necessitated a very sharp curve with a limit of 15mph. The only other station before Skegness, Havenhouse, seemed to be in the middle of nowhere, but loaded very large quantities of sugar beet and also saw many anglers in the summer. In 1951 there were ten trains a day over the branch, with some through workings to Lincoln and Grantham, and occasionally to Peterborough, Derby and Nottingham. By the late 1950s well over 100 trains a day were using the branch on summer Saturdays. The LNER had built extra sidings just before the war to cope with this demand, and had progressively enlarged the station. In 1958 it had one single-sided and three double-sided terminal platforms, only two being roofed, but with a spacious covered concourse linked directly to the bus station where connections were available to Butlin's holiday camp two miles away.

For many people the celebrated 'Jolly Fisherman' had come to symbolise Skegness. On 13 February 1908 artist John Hassall sold an oil painting for £12 to the Great Northern Railway Company which depicted a smiling fisherman bounding along a beach. Coupled with the slogan 'Skegness is so bracing' it has proved to be a powerful and enduring advertisement ever since! In 1934 Hassall was presented with a statuette of the 'Jolly Fisherman' in recognition of his services, and they were subsequently given to a number of famous people who visited the resort, such as Clement Attlee, Billy Butlin and Bob Monkhouse. In 1935 the LNER presented the original painting to the local council, which gave it pride of place in the Town Hall. It is ironic that no copies of the original poster seem to have survived, and also that the artist didn't visit Skegness until 28 years after producing it; when he did so at the age of 69 he was fêted and given a free pass to all the town's attractions. Hassall died in 1943 aged 80. British Railways and the local council continued to use the fisherman for publicity purposes, and the council recently bought the copyright.

The line to Mablethorpe started life as a branch from Louth; some years later the branch to Sutton was built from Willoughby, leaving only a short gap to be filled in to complete the loop. It enjoyed a good service of diesel multiple units in the late 1950s, with through workings on Saturdays from a variety of other places such as Nottingham, Derby and Leicester Belgrave Road. In spite of this the line was selected for closure by Dr Beeching – probably on the grounds that all this traffic was highly seasonal; in 1961 it collected 102,523 tickets, of which 62,000 were in July and August. Although closed for goods in 1964 the passenger service survived until 1970. The line between Mablethorpe and Louth closed completely at the end of 1960, and all goods services over the rest of the loop went in 1964. Mablethorpe and Sutton-on-Sea retained their passenger services, run as a branch from Willoughby, until 1970.

The final branch of the East Lincolnshire group was that from Coningsby Junction (just to the south of Woodhall Junction) to Bellwater Junction, which had had an interesting history, but was little more than a cut-off for Lincoln-Skegness trains, which were the only traffic by 1958, although they generally called at all sta-

Above right:

In July 1955 ex-Great Central Class A5 No 69819 passes Boston Loco (40F) with a local working to Grantham.
Les Perrin

Right:

On 11 October 1951 'J68' No 68658 shunts in Boston goods yard.
Les Perrin

tions along the line. Again, the line was one of Dr Beeching's victims.

The Great Northern's 'main lines' in Lincolnshire were really the East Lincs line, 78.5 miles from Peterborough to Grimsby, and the joint line from Spalding to Doncaster. In the summer of 1958 it supported a very respectable service of stopping and fast trains, some running over its whole length and others over parts of it, perhaps *en route* for some of the branches and destinations already mentioned. The 5.49am up from Grimsby called at most stations on the line, reaching Peterborough North at 8.42am. It was followed by the 6.50am, which carried a restaurant-buffet car and worked through to King's Cross (154.25 miles distant), reached at 10.38am. This called only at Louth, Alford Town, Willoughby (connection from Mablethorpe), Firsby (connection from Skegness), Boston and Spalding. There was then a stopper from Grimsby to Louth, another from Louth to Willoughby via Mablethorpe, a stopper from Louth to Peterborough (which missed Firsby), and then the through restaurant-buffet service from Cleethorpes to King's Cross, off Grimsby at 8.48am, and so on. During the day the line also saw through workings between Lincoln and Peterborough, Skegness to Peterborough and Mablethorpe to Nottingham, as well as a series of other local and fast trains. No matter – Dr Beeching got most of it in the end, with one or two exceptions. Although the Skegness branch was cited for closure, it survived via the south curve, Firsby station

closing as planned. Trains continued to run from Boston, and across from there to Sleaford, the main line to Spalding being closed. However, it was also intended to close the Spalding-Werrington Junction section, but keep open the GN&GE joint line between Spalding and March. In the event the opposite happened: Peterborough-Spalding survived and March-Spalding closed in 1982, although its intermediate stations had gone long before. Louth closed to passengers, with the rest of the line, except as noted above, in 1970 and survived for freight until December 1980, worked from Grimsby.

To the west of the ECML the line from Grantham to Nottingham Victoria was another Great Northern one, although west of Netherfield it had been transferred into the London Midland Region. It was one of the last to retain steam haulage on local services, and had a frequent local service right through the 1950s, with some trains worked through from Derby Friargate, although the majority started at Nottingham Victoria, then calling at London Road (High Level). Nottingham, of course, also had its own suburban line, and trains from Derby could also avoid the city completely by running via Gedling. Stations on the line from Grantham included Bottesford, also served by the occasional working from Leicester Belgrave Road to Mablethorpe, where large quantities of ironstone were fed in from the Denton branch via Belvoir Junction: 550,000 tons in 1960, and 617,175 the following year. The branch also generated a great deal of sugar beet

Left:
'V2' No 60948 arrives at Lincoln Central with a train for Colchester on 20 June 1960. This would have been routed via the Joint line as far as March.
Dennis C. Ovenden

Below:
On the Lincolnshire coast Theddlethorpe station two weeks before closure is deserted except for a bike and a ladder. Situated on the loop from Louth to Mablethorpe it could be a windswept place, loaded little goods but a few livestock, and closed completely in December 1960.
Douglas Thompson

traffic. The station had staggered platforms, with its main buildings on the down side, together with a large goods yard and warehouse. Elton & Orston, 2.5 miles further on, needed only two porter-signalmen to cover all the duties, with its main traffics being mushroom spawn inwards and mushrooms outwards. Bingham was an important town with two nearby air force camps which generated a great deal of traffic in goods and personnel. The surrounding area was also renowned for its Stilton cheese, large quantities being sent away by rail. The station also had the capacity to store 35,000 sacks which were hired out to local farmers. The new colliery at Cotgrave also caused much activity, including the building of a five-mile branch line. Netherfield & Colwick, 19.25 miles from Grantham, had been badly damaged during the war and was rebuilt in 1961, with modern office accommodation and a new signalbox. It handled large quantities of freight traffic: 70,000 wagonloads of coal in 1961, with sugar beet pulp, iron, steel and general merchandise outwards, and in 1961 28,000 wagons inward, mainly sugar beet, petrol and oil.

55

Above:

Algarkirk & Sutterton was a station on the East Lincs line between Boston and Spalding, seen here in 1950, and showing the care that was lavished on its appearance and gardens by its staff.
Locomotive & General 23563

Left:

Firsby station retained its Great Northern air until the end, and even the diesel multiple unit scarcely detracts from it, on 24 August 1964. This Lincoln-Skegness train reversed at Firsby, and parcels are loaded while it waits.
P. G. Moore

Above right:

'B12/3' No 61565 makes a spirited departure from Skegness on 10 July 1955 with a return excursion to Grantham.
J. Cupit

Right:

Class B1 No 61141 passes Sleaford with steam to spare whilst in charge of a Derby-Mablethorpe special on 29 August 1964
R. Madley

Above:
'J6' No 64251 works tender-first leaving Peterborough East as it heads for the North station with a breakdown train in September 1960.
John C Baker

Right:
Class C12 No 67376 of New England shed (35A) stands outside Stamford East with the 2.50pm for Essendine on 2 March 1957, two days before the station officially lost its passenger service.
P. H. Wells

CHAPTER 5 The North Eastern Lines

The North Eastern Region of British Railways originally comprised the former Northern Area of the LNER, which corresponded to a large extent to the territory of the former North Eastern Railway. It included some parts of the old North British system where they were south of the border, and later came also to embrace parts of the former London Midland & Scottish Railway, especially in the area to the west of Leeds and Bradford, where it took control of the former Midland lines almost as far as Skipton. All of Bradford came under its sway, as did the former Lancashire & Yorkshire route as far as Hebden Bridge. A few parts were lost: Kirkby Stephen and westwards went to the LMR, and there were many adjustments to the boundary with the Eastern Region before the two were amalgamated.

The most important of the region's lines was undoubtedly the East Coast main line, which ran through its territory from Shaftholme Junction to the Scottish border. It had several other main lines, or shares in them, notably Doncaster-Leeds (Doncaster was in Eastern Region territory), Leeds-Selby-Hull, York-Scarborough, and the lines to Teesside: Stockton, Middlesbrough, Hartlepool and the coastal route to Sunderland. It inherited a great many very rural branch lines throughout its area, some quite idyllic such as Weardale or Middleton-in-Teesdale, although this often belied their importance as generators of industrial traffic, mainly through quarrying or mining. There were great flows of freight traffic which had been the backbone of the NER, making it one of Britain's soundest railways financially, and which continued to bolster the region until changing indus-

trial practices, recession and competition from the roads combined to erode it. Tyneside and Teesside received huge quantities of coal and ores; Consett was a byword for heavy trains slogging up to the iron works, while long trains of limestone trundled off the Weardale and Wensleydale branches.

Eryholme was the junction for the Richmond branch, a busy line with up to 13 trains each way daily, and a good Sunday service as late as the winter of 1958-9, although it did not lose its passenger service for another ten years. Catterick Bridge station did a very good business with the military camps at Catterick, and there were some very intensive workings of special trains over the branch to deal with leave traffic, mostly handled at Richmond. On the big holidays – Christmas, Easter, Whitsun, August Bank Holiday – huge numbers of personnel required transport within a very short time. The procedure was for the military authorities first to ascertain the destinations of all personnel, so that the appropriate trains and rolling stock could be ordered. Departures for Leeds and Lancashire, London and the Eastern Counties (possibly in quadruplicate), Glasgow, Liverpool, North Wales, Birmingham and Bristol were needed, and buses from United Automobile Services were provided between the camp and Richmond station. Tickets or travel warrants had already been issued before personnel reached the station, and their accounting took a great deal of time for the station staff. The whole operation was scheduled to take about three hours, empty stock being worked in from various stabling points. Departures from Richmond were at about 20min intervals, each train being 11 or 12

Left:
Darlington Bank Top from the road in 1952. The streets are still gas-lit and the trolleybuses are still running, but cars are conspicuous by their absence.
Locomotive & General 26639

coaches and seating up to 700 troops. Richmond station also handled chertstone, mined some 15 miles away and transported thence by road motor, and in the late 1940s just over 500 tons a year were forwarded at a value of nearly £600 to the railway.

The line from Malton to Driffield had also closed to passengers at an early date, in June 1950, but was retained for freight. Its only engineering work of any note was Burdale Tunnel at 1746yd long; its stations were close to the villages that they served except for Sledmere, which was three miles away and the most important! In the mid-1950s it saw a pick-up freight only on Tuesdays and Thursdays, plus the occasional excursion to Whitby. In February 1958 all roads in the area were blocked and the train – nicknamed locally the 'Malton Dodger' – returned, bringing milk, bread, meat and other groceries to the villagers, and picking up 1,360 churns of milk for the factory at Driffield. The closure of Burdale Quarry had been the beginning of the end for the line, and its value in emergency could not save it: it closed to all traffic on 20 October 1958. Some other branches closed to passengers relatively early in British Railways days, such as that from Pilmoor to Gilling and Pickering in February 1953, although the occasional trains did continue to run. For example, at the request of local people, excursions ran to York and Leeds for shopping and football at Christmas 1954, from Kirkbymoorside, Nawton, Helmsley, Gilling and Coxwold.

Market Weighton was served by lines from York, Selby, Driffield and Hull. It was thus remarkably well placed for access to some of the main towns of Yorkshire, itself being a market town in the middle of a fertile agricultural district. To the east and north-east the Yorkshire Wolds rolled away, but it was much flatter on the plain westwards to Selby and York. On the latter's light soils root crops thrived: potatoes, carrots, parsnips and sugar beet, all sent away by train, whilst machinery, fertilisers and feedstuffs came inwards. At the station, provided with modern canopies, there was a prefabricated warehouse for the storage of cattle and poultry feed. It hired out huge quantities of sacks, nearly 40,000 in 1954, with a very beneficial effect on revenue. There were four nursery gardens in the immediate vicinity which generated a considerable flow of passenger-rated parcels traffic.

A daily pick-up goods operated between Market Weighton and York, Selby and Malton; the station and its goods yard, staffed by a foreman and two porters handling nearly 2,000 wagons in 1954. Additional traffic came from the Air Ministry depot outside the station, and a large motor engineering business which employed over 100 staff. The three water columns at the station were supplied by St Helen's spring, two miles away, which was owned and administered by the British Transport Commission, although drinking water came from the town mains. The station was a centre for road delivery, and also oversaw the distribution of signal lamp oil to nine other stations. Apart from the extensive freight traffic already described, the station saw up to eighty trains for Filey Holiday Camp, Bridlington and Scarborough pass through on summer Saturdays, and also empty stock trains from Hull, which, with a busy level crossing at the west end of the station, gave rise to some problems. The stationmaster at Market Weighton was also responsible for Londesborough, next on the line to York.

Market Weighton's passenger service was twofold. One operated between Selby and Bridlington, and in summer 1946 amounted to four trains each way on weekdays, one being a Leeds-Bridlington through service calling only at Market

Below:
Shildon station on the line from Darlington; a dmu for Crook runs in on 27 April 1962. Behind the train the yard is a hive of activity – today it is deserted and overgrown.
I. S. Carr

Above:

The Masham branch, from Melmerby on the Leeds Northern line between Harrogate and Northallerton, had closed to passengers in 1931, but retained its goods service. On 15 August 1960 Class 08 No D3313 heads the daily train over Millbank crossing.
R. E. James-Robertson

Weighton on the line; the others were all-stations. By 1955 this had been reduced to two each way, the intermediate stations all having closed to passengers in September 1954. By 1958 there was just one Bridlington-Selby train a day, with another from Bridlington and terminating; in the other direction there were two trains, one being a through Leeds-Bridlington service which did not run on Saturdays. The Hull-York service was rather better, with eight each way in 1946, some omitting the smaller stations. Twelve years later it was still much the same; still no Sunday trains, and again with some of the small stations, notably Cherry Burton and Kipling Cotes, having a very sparse service. This seemingly prosperous station was not destined to survive, however, and all the lines serving Market Weighton were slated for closure by Dr Beeching. The Hull-York trains were diverted via Selby (there had always been some via that route), and trains from Leeds could reach Bridlington via Scarborough or Hull. The axe finally fell on 29 November 1965 when passenger services were withdrawn, goods having finished at the start of the month. The station site is now a housing estate.

Wetherby's situation paralleled that of Market Weighton in some ways. Both stations were junctions on secondary lines or branches, situated in small country towns in Yorkshire. Wetherby's railways offered direct trains to Harrogate, Leeds and Church Fenton, with connections to York and further afield available at the latter. Trains ran between Church Fenton and Leeds via Wetherby, which was rather a roundabout route, or Harrogate and Leeds, which was relatively direct. Stopping trains on the latter took only slightly longer than via Horsforth, but there were a number of non-stop workings on that route as well.

The goods and passenger stations were at opposite ends of the town, about a mile apart, the former being on the line from Church Fenton, the latter on the Leeds line, and both were supervised by the same station-master. The South box was open continuously in 1960 for the passage of freight trains working from Starbeck (Harrogate) to Neville Hill, Leeds. There was also a station for the racecourse which was opened for the principal meetings, the main ones being at Easter and Whitsun. Combined rail and admission tickets were issued, most passengers coming from Leeds and other stations in the West Riding.

Traffic at the goods station included steel girders and angles from a local firm of agricultural engineers specialising in Dutch barns. There were considerable livestock forwardings from the local auction mart, and cattle feed and cement were stored at the station. Sack hire, as with many country stations, was an important activity. Miscellaneous goods traffic handled at the passenger station included the products from a local bulb farm and other nurseries, and an unusual traffic was curd to Leeds Market. The bulk of the passenger receipts was derived from the naval training grounds at Wetherby, there being 600 personnel always in residence at HMS *Ceres*. The training courses typically ran only for six weeks so there was a high turnover of personnel, and there

61

was considerable traffic in home leave as well as all the various items of baggage, stores and educational material; special trains were run at holiday times – Easter, Christmas and so on. Wennington school also generated traffic on a smaller scale, having about 100 boarders from all over the country. In the summer 1946 timetable there were only three through trains, all stoppers, between Church Fenton and Leeds via Wetherby, with an extra two on Saturdays. A further three ran through from Harrogate, but there were also a number to each destination starting at Wetherby. By November 1958 the service from Church Fenton was down to one a day, still with three from Harrogate, which represented a deterioration from the previous year. In neither case was it possible to get back direct from Wetherby to Church Fenton, the only train stopping short at Tadcaster. Not surprisingly the services were listed by Dr Beeching, and the passenger service was withdrawn from 6 January 1964, goods following from 4 April 1966.

Although the North Eastern Railway's mainstay had always been its very heavy traffic in coal and other minerals, it and its successors in the LNER and British Railways had numerous rural lines; many of them had once originated much of that mineral traffic. The trans-Pennine route from Carlisle was one such, its principal intermediate station being Hexham. Operationally it had been the junction for both the branch to Allendale and the North British line to Redesmouth and Riccarton Junction, on the Waverley route. This, and other ex-NBR lines south of the border, were included with the North Eastern Region at nationalisation, although north of the border they went into the new Scottish Region. Allendale lost its passenger service soon after the grouping, but trains continued to work over the other branch until closure in 1955, when Hexham still had two cattle markets and needed between 2,500 and 3,000 cattle wagons a year to handle the traffic. It booked some 90,000 passengers annually, and

Below:
An empty ore train from Consett coasts down through Beamish in April 1964, headed by Standard '9F' No 92065.
W. J. V. Anderson

Right:
On 20 August 1966 Class Q6 0-8-0 No 63394 starts a coal train for Consett at South Pelaw.
M. Dunnett

Far right:
Standard '9F' No 92064 blasts through Beamish with a loaded iron ore train from Tyne Dock to Consett on 19 September 1964.
M. Dunnett

then enjoyed a good service, at least half-hourly from Newcastle in the morning and evening peaks, and hourly at other times. Some trains ran via North Wylam, but most went via Wylam itself. A service westward to Carlisle operated about every two hours, some of these being quite fast, calling only at Hexham and Haltwhistle on the way. The Alston branch saw only six trains on weekdays, with a late one on Saturday evenings as well.

The North Eastern went across Stainmore summit from Barnard Castle with its lines to Tebay and Penrith, which diverged at Kirkby Stephen. Belah viaduct, five miles or so from there was one of the wonders of the railway world, having been designed by Thomas Bouch (of Tay Bridge fame), and lasting much longer than that ill-fated edifice. The Tebay service had finished in 1952, but the line to Appleby and Penrith outlasted it by ten years, the final passenger trains running on Saturday 20 January 1962, when the intermediate stations lost their service. Track was to be lifted immediately between Tees Valley Junction (one mile west of Barnard Castle) and Merrygill box, one mile east of Kirkby Stephen; also from Kirkby Stephen to Tebay, and from Appleby East to Clifton Moor, near the junction with the former LNWR main line to the north of Shap. The line from Appleby East to Merrygill, with a connection to the LMR at the former was to be retained, as was the short section from Eden Valley Junction to Clifton Moor. There had been a long and bitter fight to retain the lines, part of the North Eastern Region's strategy having been to divert freight traffic away from them and via Newcastle and Carlisle. Closure was estimated to save some

Left:

The empty stock of race specials waits on the line to Tadcaster at Wetherby South at Whitsun 1962. The line to the left goes to Wetherby station and Harrogate. The locomotives are 'Crab' No 42762 on a Bradford train, and 'B16' No 61429 on a Leeds City working.

J. M. Rayner

Above:
Class D49/2 No 62738 *The Zetland* of Starbeck shed calls at Collingham Bridge on 13 October 1956 with the 12.30pm Saturdays-only from Harrogate to Leeds via Wetherby.
M. Mitchell

£103,274 per year, and £257,000 would be realised from recovered material. Additionally around £45-50,000 would be saved in capital expenditure at Kirkby Stephen. Although the re-routeing of the freight traffic took place from 4 July 1960, disagreements between the North Eastern and North Western Transport Consultative Committees resulted in further delays to the closure: a situation echoed in the battle many years later over the Settle & Carlisle line. In this case the North Eastern committee eventually assented, and closure then came quickly. Although services had been dieselised, the last train was in fact a steam-hauled special organised by the RCTS.

A branch line of very different character which had become part of the North Eastern Region was that from Keighley to Oxenhope. Keighley had once been served by the Great Northern's branch from Queensbury, near Bradford, passenger trains running into the former Midland station, whilst it had its own goods station. The steeply-graded Midland branch to Oxenhope also served Haworth, famous for its connections with the Brontë sisters, the junction with the GN being between Ingrow and Keighley. In winter 1955-6 it enjoyed a good service of ten trains each weekday, with five extra on Saturdays, including the usual late-night trains. A day return ticket cost 1s 2d (about 6p) all the way, or 11d (4.5p) to Haworth. Diesel services were introduced on 13 June 1960, it having been the last steam-operated branch left on the region; this left Keighley depot with only one steam locomotive, a '3F' 0-6-0 for working the branch goods. Having already been proposed for closure it was hoped that economies would result; however, the service was withdrawn in 1961, the last passenger trains running on Saturday 30 December, with freight scheduled for withdrawal on and from Monday 18 June 1962. The subsequent story is, of course, well known.

Another rural North Eastern line was that out to Hawes, with the junction at Northallerton. Leeming Bar, 5.25 miles from the junction, was a small station at one end of the double track section to Bedale, and so had two platforms. Leeming aerodrome was nearby, and aeroplane parts were an everyday traffic. In 1951 the Vale of Mowbray bacon factory sent out enough bacon each Monday for 3,000 people's rations, and also consigned cartons of meat pies, sausages, etc. The station also handled agricultural implements and sent cut flowers to the markets at Newcastle, Darlington and Leeds. Leyburn was another station on the same line, some twelve miles to the west. It had a thriving livestock mart and sent away over 16,000 head of livestock from its station at the same time. Other stations in this area did not have such a regular traffic, but saw great peaks in October, with the sheep sales and cattle fairs.

Many stations which may not have had one large obvious source of goods traffic did have other smaller flows; smallholdings, nursery gardens or small-stock stud farms all consigned small loads which made a valuable contribution to railway revenues. One of the more unusual of these in Wensleydale was 'bluestalks', a type of edible fungus which grew especially in fields of stubble after harvest time. It was said that, in keeping with the old proverb that 'the early bird catches the worm', many collectors would be out at first light, and some were even said to sleep out in the fields or gather them by torch-light! They were sent

away in 'chips', which were small wooden baskets weighing 7lb securely covered with brown paper, to places such as Sheffield. Pickering was another centre noted for this traffic, and the location of the best fields was a jealously-guarded secret often handed down from father to son. Evening trains through to destination were preferred for despatch since it speeded the journey by obviating transfers, and it was the practice for the sending station to wire ahead so that the traffic could be handled as expeditiously as possible. It was all to little effect: passenger services on the Wensleydale line ended in April 1954, goods continued until 1965, and the quarries at Redmire kept the branch open until very recently. There is the possibility that this line will also be preserved.

One of the other effects of the economies on rural services was the destaffing of stations. On the Hornsea and Withernsea branches (from Hull Paragon) it took place from 4 January 1962, and affected all the stations except Hornsea Bridge, Hornsea Town and Withernsea, although it was announced that clerks would attend some stations on certain mornings in the holiday season. Both branches had enjoyed a good service, including Sundays, but the economies could not save them: Dr Beeching recommended them for closure, and they duly finished passenger services together on 19th October 1964.

The routes between Middlesbrough and Whitby formed an interesting group. There were three of them: via Battersby and Grosmont; via Guisborough and Loftus – both used all year round; and via Redcar and Loftus, used in the summer only. The lines via Loftus involved the long coastal stretch via Staithes and Sandsend, with several viaducts and tunnels, and in the 1950s these were becoming expensive to maintain, requiring considerable renewals. It was therefore decided to close the line between Loftus and Whitby West Cliff, and this was done on 5 May 1958.

All remaining traffic was to be worked by the present route, involving reversal at Battersby.

The coast line branched from the Whitby-Pickering route at Bog Hall junction, just outside Whitby Town, having passed under the viaduct carrying the line from Scarborough and Robin Hood's Bay. It then climbed up at 1 in 50 to Prospect Hill Junction to join the Scarborough line, and then into West Cliff station. Soon after this it started falling at 1 in 60 towards Sandsend, where the single platform on the landward side was reputed to be nearer the beach than any other. Before this it crossed Upgang and Newholm Beck viaducts, and then, approaching the station, East Row and Sandsend viaducts, the latter almost at the end of the platform. This was cut into the cliff, which then fell away to the beach, and was a favourite location for publicity shots of the railway. Shortly after the station, the line – keeping on the cliffs – ran into Sandsend tunnel (1,657yd), on a gradient of 1 in 57. Kettleness tunnel (308yd) followed shortly after, both having been built so that the line could be taken further inland rather than kept on the edge of the cliffs. Later falls showed the wisdom of this course, although some work had already been done on the seaward route. Still climbing hard, trains reached the summit after a further 1.5 miles before dropping down into Staithes, where the best-known of the viaducts was situated, with the station immediately to the north.

65

Left:

Church Fenton was a busy station on the former York & North Midland Railway, and was an important junction with lines to Harrogate via Tadcaster and to Leeds branching off. In this view, taken on 28 March 1959 the 3.10pm York to Leeds pauses in platform 3, headed by the last of the BR Standard Class 5s, No 73171.

M. Mitchell

Below left:

The 2.30pm Leeds-Scarborough pulls away from Church Fenton under the gaze of two young boys on 27 February 1960.

M. Mitchell

Staithes viaduct was 700ft long and 162ft high, with 16 piers each consisting of two tubular iron columns filled with cement and braced together. It was so exposed that a wind gauge was situated at the south end of the viaduct, which rang a bell in the signalbox; trains were prohibited from crossing when wind pressure exceeded 28lbs per square foot. There then followed another stiff climb for some 2.5 miles to Grinkle tunnel, the station there having been closed when war broke out in 1939. Loftus station then followed, the section onwards suffering greatly from mining subsidence. The line from Middlesbrough was to have been terminated here, although the passenger service lasted exactly two years longer than that along the line to Whitby, closing in May 1960. Goods traffic finished in 1963, although the line was subsequently relaid for ironstone traffic. The whole of this area was full of these workings, and indeed the North Eastern had purchased the reserves under Brotton station from the mining company in order to prevent subsidence. Much income was generated for the NER by its carriage, and this activity continued into the British Railways era and up to the present.

Trains to Middlesbrough via Guisborough called at the latter by reversal, since it was a terminal station on a short spur. From Middlesbrough they ran into the station and then reversed back to the junction before continuing their journey. Other trains (latterly only two a day each way) ran via Redcar, and did not call at Saltburn since it too was on a spur, facing Middlesbrough. Locomotives working the trains on these lines came either from Whitby or Middlesbrough sheds, and were usually Class 'A8' 4-6-2 tanks, 'L1' 2-6-4 tanks, LMR and Standard Class 4 tanks and LMR Class 4 or Standard Class 3 2-6-0s. In summer other classes from other sheds appeared, such as 'B1s' or 'A5s' from Scarborough, Darlington or Stockton.

Not all of the North Eastern's secondary lines were rural, of course. Saltburn station was one of the busier North Eastern Region ones on the east coast, after the great ports. Saltburn performed a number of functions in the Teesside area – as the 'lungs' for its workers, as a desirable place to live, and later as an industrial centre in its own right, and as such it generated much traffic for the railways. Originally patronized by wealthy businessmen who travelled first class to their offices daily, it was assiduously cultivated by the North Eastern, and the lower promenade retaining sea wall and two slipways were built of old Stockton & Darlington square stone sleepers. In the early 1950s up to 66,000 passengers were being booked annually, with 273,000 tickets being received, which excluded season ticket holders. In the summer season, lasting about three months, the station would see through trains to Blackpool, Manchester and Glasgow, with a through train each weekday between Saltburn and London. An unusual

Below:

A diesel multiple unit forming the 6.6pm Saturdays-only Harrogate to Leeds City via Wetherby pulls away from Bardsey in June 1963. In spite of the large number of vans in the siding the station was targeted by Dr Beeching and closed six months later to all traffic.

J. M. Rayner

freight traffic was in lobsters, received from Staithes and forwarded to London and the continent. Heavy freight from Skinningrove Ironworks and the Cleveland Ironstone mines also passed Saltburn West on their way to Teesside, a great deal of this traffic being destined for the Newport Yards, between Thornaby and Middlesbrough, which handled 5-6,000 wagons daily in the early 1950s. Saltburn had its own motive power depot (51K).

At holiday times the lines to the coast would carry very heavy traffic. Redcar races were a big attraction, with visitors coming from as far away as Sheffield and Newcastle, and both resorts had miles of sandy beaches. Much forward planning was needed on the part of the railway authorities, who first needed to know from local firms what leave was being granted and when. They also needed to take account of the precise date when Easter or Whitsun fell, since the weather could make a big difference to likely destinations and demand for travel. Likely requirements for coaching stock, locomotives and crews could then be worked out, bearing in mind that normal services were not to be disrupted. The main flow on Teesside was from Darlington, Stockton, Thornaby and Middlesbrough to Redcar and Saltburn, these two handling up to 25,000 people daily, and with extra traffic also from Bishop Auckland. Passengers from there would normally have had to change at Darlington, but it was arranged to have some trains run through to the coast on holiday weekends. Working out paths through Darlington station could be a problem since the main line service was also augmented.

On the other hand, Darlington Market also proved to be a big draw on Easter and Whit Mondays, and provided a counter-flow inland. Special one-off events might also occur in particular years: in 1952 there were big cyclists' meets at Barnard Castle and Richmond, and an excursion was run from Saltburn via Darlington to Richmond for this. The Middleton-in-Teesdale-Darlington train, normally a push-pull working, was converted to a normal steam train to give extra capacity. The interval service between Newcastle and Middlesbrough via the coast had the interval lengthened during the slack periods of the day, when certain main line through workings took up the spare paths. A push-pull train gave connections out of these at Stockton for Middlesbrough, and again would be converted to a normal train at peak holiday times.

Whitby trains were normally kept clear of the Saltburn line, although some were run that way in summer. This, combined with heavy passenger traffic, meant that some freight traffic for Skinningrove (which would normally have run via Redcar) might have to be routed via the more steeply graded line through Hutton Gate, which necessitated provision of a banker between Middlesbrough and Nunthorpe. Other goods services might be curtailed, and goods lines used for stabling passenger stock, and their crews freed for passenger work. A shuttle service would be run between Stockton and Redcar, calling at all stations, and any other extras would run without stopping to Redcar. The chronic shortage of rolling stock on the whole of British Railways in the early 1950s caused considerable problems, and all available coaches would be pressed into service, including some venerable pre-grouping examples. Extra station staff were also drafted in to assist at places like Redcar and Saltburn.

On Tyneside the electric trains performed much the same function, although they also offered an intensive suburban service for commuters into Newcastle. They were inaugurated in 1904 to Whitley Bay and Tynemouth, trains soon running a circular service from Central to Central, and were supplemented in 1938 when the LNER electrified the line to South Shields. The lines provided an invaluable outlet for people to get to the fresh air of the seaside, and one of the features of the services was the cheap evening trips, available after 6.00pm on weekdays and 4.00pm on Sundays. However, the South Shields service was abandoned by BR in 1963 and Whitley Bay in 1967, both being replaced by a service of diesel multiple units, mainly on the grounds that the infrastructure had deteriorated to the extent that renewal was not economic, and it certainly presented a fairly depressing picture to the intending traveller. The Ponteland branch, with its extension to Darras Hall, had also been intended as a part of the electrified network, but this was not done and it was operated by a steam railcar until closure to passengers in 1929, although retained for goods traffic until 1967. After a period of diesel operation by British Rail, the Tyneside loop and the South Shields line were taken over by the local PTE, re-electrified and incorporated into the Tyne & Wear Metro.

Below:

Class A4 Pacific No 60019 *Bittern* arrives at Eaglescliffe with the 3.50pm Sundays-only Newcastle to King's Cross on 12 May 1957. The train has been diverted because of engineering work on the main line.
B. K. B. Green

Above:
The 4.45pm fitted freight from West Hartlepool to York crosses the River Tees at Yarm, on the Leeds Northern main line. 'K1' No 62004 is in charge on 20 May 1965.
John M. Boyes

Left:
Two ex-NER 0-8-0s shunt at Billingham South sidings on 6 July 1957.
H. Gordon Tidey

69

Above:
On 17 July 1960 Dearness Valley junction, just south of Durham, sees 'Q6' No 63448 heading a freight from the Blackhill area on to the Bishop Auckland line. The main line curves away on the far left, and the Waterhouses branch on the right.
I. S. Carr

Left:
Class G5 0-4-4T No 67258 storms away from Cox Green with the 1.42pm Durham to Sunderland train on 28 March 1957. This service was withdrawn in May 1964.
I. S. Carr

Above right:
'WD' 2-8-0 No 90417 heads the 11.5am West Hartlepool to York coal train past Newburn junction, West Hartlepool, on 2 June 1967.
John M. Boyes

Right:
In contrast to the long trains of coal or iron ore Class Q6 No 63458 and brake van head south along the coast at Ryhope, Co Durham on 28 October 1966. The bridge bears the initials 'LSSR', meaning Londonderry Seaham & Sunderland Railway, which later became part of the North Eastern.
I. S. Carr

Left:

'V3' No 67688 calls at Penshaw with an up parcels train on the evening of 5 September 1960.
Colin P. Walker

Below left:

On 22 August 1961 Bo-Bo electric locomotive No 26500 is seen from the platform at Manors station, wearing North Eastern Railway livery. It has just emerged from Trafalgar yard, whose overhead wires are clearly visible on the right, and is waiting to cross to the down line to gain access to Heaton depot. These locomotives could take power either from overhead or from the third rail.
I. S. Carr

Right:

Class B1 No 61034 *Chiru* heads through Manors on 12 August 1961 with a summer Saturday express for Scotland.
I. S. Carr

Below:

On the line to Carlisle, Blaydon was a large and important station and a junction for the lines to Tow Law and Bishop Auckland, Blackhill and Durham, and also to Scotswood. This view was taken looking in the down direction in 1951.
Locomotive & General 25657

CHAPTER 6

North Eastern Motive Power

The North Eastern Railway, as one of the most important in the country, had had a large stock of locomotives, handing over 2,005 to the LNER at the Grouping. Of these, 1,128 survived to be taken into British Railways stock in 1948, with just under 900 surviving to 1954. Many had been replaced by more modern machines, especially on the front-line duties such as the ECML: for example, the Raven 'Pacifics' had been withdrawn in 1937-8, largely being replaced by Gresley's 'A1s'. Both the 2- and 3-cylinder 'Atlantic' classes became extinct in 1948, while many of the 'D20' 4-4-0s survived on secondary work into the mid-1950s, running between Selby and York, Hull, Leeds and Doncaster; they also operated out of Alnmouth Junction on Newcastle-Alnwick services.

Passenger tank locomotives continued to be represented by the 'G5' 0-4-4s, which covered much of the branch line work in the area, and indeed elsewhere – they were to be found as far afield as the Great North of Scotland and in East Anglia. The heavy 'A8' 4-6-2 tanks worked on some of the heavily-graded coastal routes such as Scarborough-Whitby, Newcastle-Sunderland-Middlesbrough, and also Darlington-Saltburn and Malton-Whitby. The 'B16' 4-6-0s, either in original or one of their rebuilt forms were mostly concentrated at York and Neville Hill, and did sterling work on the heavy holiday trains between York and Scarborough.

Freight tender locomotives survived well. The 'Q7' 0-8-0s, with their tractive effort of nearly 37,000lb were mainly used on the heavy iron ore workings between Tyne Dock and Consett until replaced by the Standard Class 9 2-10-0s. In 1954 there were still about 120 Class Q6s at various depots around the region, mainly on Teesside. Of the 0-6-0 tender engines the 'J26s' were concentrated in the Middlesbrough area, whilst the much larger numbers (115 in 1954) of 'J27s' were widely dispersed. The smaller 'J21s', originally built as compounds, were still used on both passenger and freight work between Darlington and Kirkby Stephen. On the tank side the powerful 'T1' 4-8-0s were used for hump shunting at the large Newport yards, whilst at the other end of the scale the tiny 'Y8' 0-4-0 survived in 1954 as the York shed pilot. The elderly 'J77s' still survived in that year, whilst the numerous 'J72s', dating originally from 1898, were to be found scattered over the whole region and beyond. They were an unusual class in that they had first been built by the North Eastern, more added by the LNER, whilst British Railways built another 28 in 1950-1.

Below:
On 29 May 1954 'B1' No 61011 *Waterbuck* is seen speeding past North Wylam junction with an afternoon express from Newcastle to Carlisle.
J. D. Smit

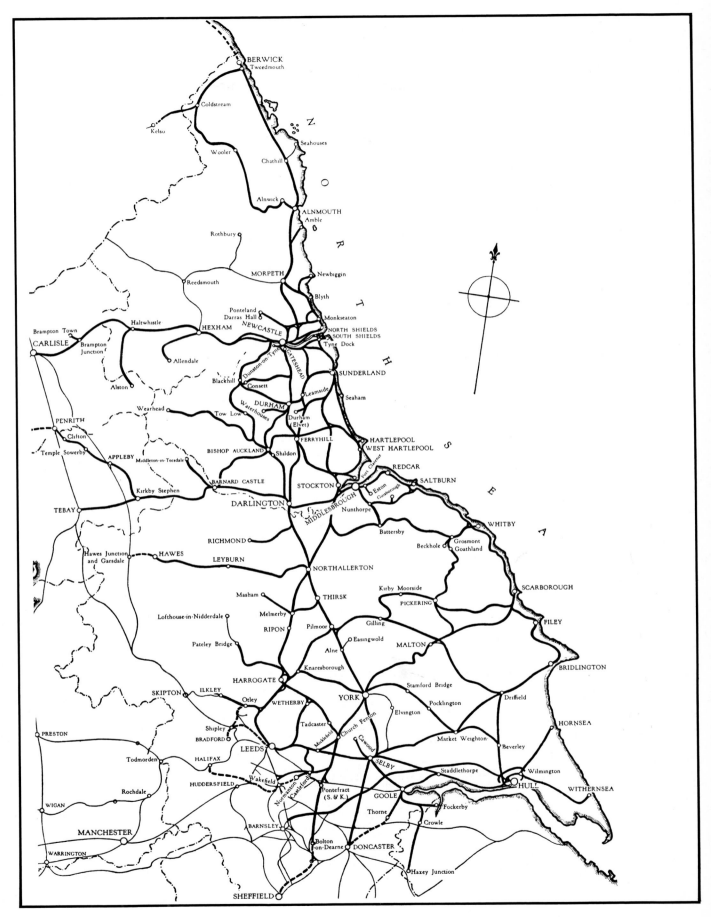

75

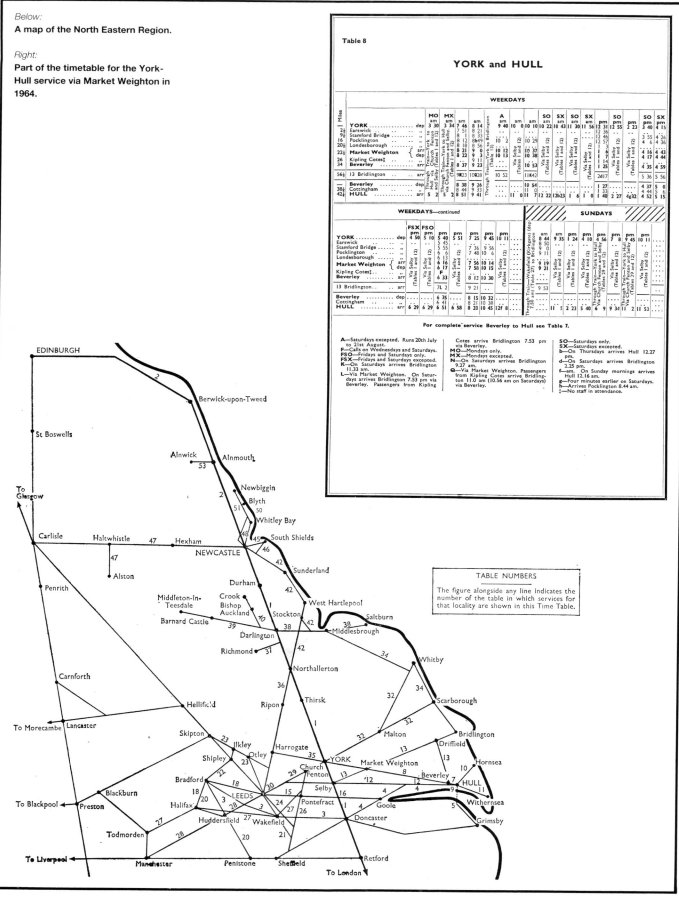

Below:

A map of the North Eastern Region.

Right:

Part of the timetable for the York-Hull service via Market Weighton in 1964.

76

Above:

Class J27 No 65825 passes Bedlington, on the former Blyth & Tyne railway, in charge of a coal train from Morpeth in August 1963 .
J. M. Rayner

Left:

On 19 March 1966 'K1' No 62011 crosses the River Alne viaduct with the 4.52pm Alnmouth to Alnwick. Although not cited by Dr Beeching the branch had closed entirely by the end of 1968.
John M. Boyes

Left:
A very fine set of North Eastern Railway lattice-post signals at Alnwick station, surviving in 1963.
Real Photographs K5545

Below:
Neville Hill 'K3' No 61869 pulls away from the platform at Hull Paragon with the 2.30pm to King's Cross on 27 August 1960.
Colin P. Walker

Right:
'V3' No 67663 stands on the stops at Hull Paragon, having run in with empty coaching stock.
Ian Allan Library

Below right:
'B1' No 61051 has just arrived at Scarborough with the 8.17am from Sheffield Victoria on 21 July 1958.
M. Mensing

Left:
'L1' No 67755 is passing Falgrave box, approaching Scarborough, with a train from Whitby on 3 August 1950, and the signalman has just collected the tablet for the single line. The tunnel was necessary to get the Whitby line through the ridge of high ground to the north of the town.
W. S. Garth

Below:
The anemometer on Staithes viaduct, connected to the nearby signalbox.
Geoffrey Oates

Bottom:
At Ravenscar station on 13 July 1957 Standard Class 4 No 80120 waits to leave for Scarborough with the 4.20pm from Whitby Town, while 'B1' No 61037 *Jairou* runs in from the single line with the 4.2pm Scarborough to Middlesbrough.
M. Mensing

Right:
On 21 July 1958 Class A8 tank No 69861 has just arrived at Whitby Town with the 4.0pm from Malton.
M. Mensing

Below right:
In August 1954 'A8' No 69886 arrives at Whitby West Cliff with a local from Whitby Town. The 1.75-mile journey was scheduled to take 6min, and only trains from the Brotton direction could call at both without reversal.
Kenneth Field

Right:
Standard Class 4 No 80118 heads the 10.28am train from York to Whitby over the level crossing and into the station at Ruswarp on 19 July 1957.
M. Mensing

Below right:
Brotton, on the coast line from Whitby to Middlesbrough, looking towards the latter. The train is seen coming off the line from Hutton Gate, the route on the right being towards Saltburn. A great deal of heavy traffic passed through Brotton on its way to Skinningrove, but it was usually routed via the coast, which was more easily graded; August 1955.
Douglas Thompson

Bottom right:
Trains pass at Battersby on 28 June 1957, and whilst one takes water there is clearly no hurry with the other.
Hugh Davies

Facing page, top:
Guisborough was a terminal station on one route to Whitby, and trains had either to reverse in or out. Here, a train for Middlesbrough stands at the platform on 26 June 1957.
Hugh Davies

Facing page, bottom:
A general view of Saltburn station taken from the signalbox on 26 June 1957; Class A8 No 69872 stands at the platform.
Hugh Davies

82

Below:

Class G5 No 67335 leaves Levisham and prepares to attack the gradient towards Goathland with a Malton-Whitby train in the 1950s.
C. Ord

Right:

An unusual view of Class B1 No 61198 as it climbs past Darnholm, between Grosmont and Goathland with the morning goods from Whitby on 4 September 1964. Both stations had lost their goods services in April, together with Levisham, but Pickering stayed open until July 1966.
John Clark

Bottom:

Class O4/8 No 63781 passes Stainforth & Hatfield, on the Grimsby-Doncaster line of the Great Central, with westbound coal empties in April 1961.
John C. Baker

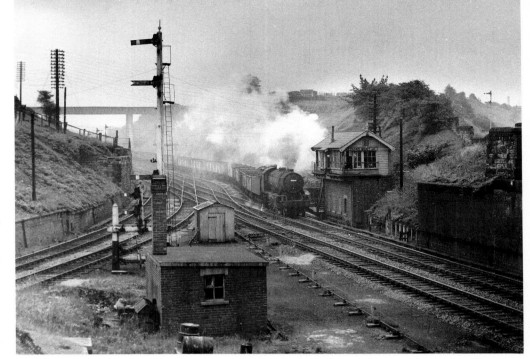

CHAPTER

7

The Great Central's Lines

The Great Central's history is too well known to bear much repetition here. Having sprung from the Manchester, Sheffield and Lincoln shire Railway at the very end of the last century, its London extension was the product of Sir Edward Watkin's international ambitions which included a second 'Eiffel Tower' at Wembley, and a first Channel Tunnel. It had turned itself from a cross-country railway with major industrial and port interests into yet another trunk route between London and the North, competing fiercely with its many rivals in the same market, principally the Midland and London & North Western. Remembered by many only for the fine line into Marylebone, it had one of the major trans-Pennine lines in the Woodhead route, and carried many thousands of tons of coal from Lancashire, Yorkshire, and the collieries of Nottinghamshire and Derbyshire. Prior to the 'rationalisation' and closure of much of the Great Central system, there were two main routes out of Marylebone, which were the Metropolitan & Great Central Joint line via Aylesbury, and the Great Western & Great Central Joint via High Wycombe. They diverged at Neasden, which was thus the obvious choice for the site of the main London area loco sheds, and came together again at Grendon Underwood junction. Aylesbury itself was further complicated by being administered by a joint committee of the other two joint committees!

Going northwards, the line served Rugby, Leicester and Loughborough, the stations there being suffixed by 'Central' for obvious reasons, but Nottingham and Sheffield both had 'Victoria' attached. At least at Nottingham this was due to the station being joint with the Great Northern, who would certainly not have swallowed the 'Central' tag; being opened in the year of the Queen's Diamond Jubilee, 'Victoria' was a good compromise. At Sheffield the Great Central was on its old territory, its original lines going across to Lincolnshire and Manchester, with the addition of the Lancashire, Derbyshire & East Coast route via Dukeries Junction. Ultimately it penetrated far to the west with its share in the Cheshire Lines Committee giving access to Merseyside, and even getting into Wales via the Wrexham, Mold & Connah's Quay line.

One of the problems of the Great Central's new main line to Marylebone was its relative lack of junctions and connections with other routes. Well-engineered and laid-out, it was ideally suited to fast running, although it could be hair-raising to run

Below:
One of the mainstays of the Great Central line: an Orgreaves-Frodingham coke train passes Brancliffe East junction on 29 August 1963
A. W. Martin

past its island platform stations at speed, with the main lines curving around them. There was interchange at some points on the line, notably Nottingham Victoria, where the Great Northern shared the joint station. Its trains travelled east-west, arriving from Grantham via London Road High Level, and joined the Great Central at Weekday Cross junction; they either diverged for Derby at Bagthorpe junction, or for Hucknall and Annesley at Bulwell Common; the latter lost its passenger services in the 1930s. There were connections with the Great Western at the London end, but more importantly at Banbury, the link from Woodford Halse seeing much through traffic between the two systems. Also near the capital the Great Central connected with the Metropolitan (LPTB) services, and the LNER later took over their working north of Rickmansworth when the line was electrified thence in 1937. This involved the acquisition by the LNER of several ex-Metropolitan locomotives, replaced after a time by 'A5' 4-6-2 tanks, in turn later displaced by 'L1' 2-6-4 tanks (hauling Gresley articulated suburban coaching sets). These were ultimately supplanted in later years by Standard Class 4 tanks in the 80xxx series.

The main line services often ran up by one route and down by the other — for example, the up 'Master Cutler' ran via the Metropolitan line, and returned via High Wycombe. The two lines were quite different in character, the Metropolitan being shared with LPTB electric services as far as Rickmansworth, and latterly had a number of speed restrictions between Harrow-on-the-Hill and Amersham. The joint line proper began at Harrow South Junction, actually to the east of the station, where the most southerly pair of tracks were the Great Central lines from Marylebone, and the other four those of the Metropolitan from Baker Street; they kept close company for a considerable way, almost from Finchley Road. Just at the west end of Harrow station the Uxbridge line burrowed under the Great Central, and the remaining pair of tracks – Metropolitan to Watford – converged, so that all traffic used just two tracks as far as Moor Park. This caused considerable congestion and delay – there were Metropoli-

tan stopping and fast trains, Great Central expresses, light engines and freight traffic on this section.

The original two stations (Pinner and Northwood) between Harrow and Rickmansworth had been supplemented by North Harrow, Northwood Hills and Moor Park & Sandy Lodge at different times, and were served by both British Railways and Metropolitan passenger services. In 1960 proposals to quadruple the line between Harrow-on-the-Hill and Moor Park were implemented, thus providing a new pair of tracks for Great Central trains, allowing them to be kept separate from the Metropolitan's Watford services. Having been undulating gently from Neasden, there was then a stiff climb, most of it at 1 in 105, between Rickmansworth and Amersham; the start from Rickmansworth was even worse, being restricted by the 1 in 90 gradient and the sharp curve, which necessitated a 25mph speed limit.

Chorley Wood & Chenies was reached part-way along this climb through chalk cuttings, and from 1962 was to be the first stop after Harrow for British Railways trains. Chalfont & Latimer station, still on the long pull up to Amersham, was a similar station, but with a bay on the up side for branch trains. Amersham had been a typical two-platform country station on the Metropolitan; development had been very much encouraged by the company. Under the electrification scheme associated with the widening it was to become the terminus of Metropolitan services from Baker Street, with its down platform acquiring an outer face. All services beyond Amersham were to be taken over by British Railways, and the stations thence to Aylesbury (Great Missenden, Wendover and Stoke Mandeville) transferred to BR. At the same time, the Chesham branch was to be electrified and its services to be taken over by London Transport.

Below:
A Bradford-Cleethorpes excursion approaches Cleethorpes Road Junction box, having passed Grimsby Docks station; 'B1' No 61297 is the train engine.
T. Booth

Left:

Chesterfield Central in July 1951, looking northward along the main platforms.

Douglas Thompson

Below left:

Staveley Works station about 1950, with everything intact: awnings on both platforms, wooden buildings; note that the track is crossed by subway.

Douglas Thompson

The line reached its first real summit just past Amersham, then dropped at 1 in 160 through beech woods in the Misbourne valley where excursion tickets for walkers had long been a popular feature at local stations. A gentler climb then followed, through Great Missenden and past Dutchmans box to Dutchmans summit, then dropping sharply again – much at 1 in 117 – through the Wendover gap to Wendover, then Stoke Mandeville and Aylesbury, 37.75 miles from Marylebone. Here there were three through roads (the down platform was an island), together with an upside bay for Metropolitan trains, with those from Princes Risborough using the outside down platform. Beyond Aylesbury, Waddesdon Manor station was closed in 1935, with the next, Quainton Road, marking the junction of the Joint line with the Great Central proper. Beyond this the line undulated gently until it reached Grendon Underwood, where it rejoined the alternative Wycombe line.

The Wycombe route was effectively much newer, with many of its stations laid out in typical Great Western style with the main lines passing between side platform loops. The GWR had planned the Acton & Wycombe line as part of its programme to shorten its line from Paddington to Birmingham, and when approached by the Great Central on the question of alternative access to Marylebone put the new line under the aegis of the joint committee. The line was much more gently graded, there being a short downhill stretch of 1 in 62 in the down line only at Northolt Junction, and further downhill sections of 1 in 100 and 1 in 88, again in the down line only, at Saunderton. Here three miles of the original single track became the down road, and the up was built new, with a uniform gradient of 1 in 167 and an 84yd tunnel; there was another, of 348yd, at White House Farm near Beaconsfield. At Northolt Junction the down Great Central line burrowed under the Great Western, with the Central line extension of London Transport later constructed alongside. This terminated at West Ruislip (Ruislip & Ickenham until 1947), where car sheds were built and where the majority of local trains to High Wycombe made their first call after Marylebone. There were water troughs just beyond the station on the level section, and beyond South Harefield halt (closed in 1931) the line started to rise gently, passing over the viaducts east of Denham, through the Golf Club platforms, the fine station at Gerrards Cross and on to the summit between Seer Green and Beaconsfield.

From High Wycombe the route had been part of the former Great Western line between Maidenhead and Princes Risborough, originally opened as a single track in 1862 as an extension of the line from Maidenhead; it later went on via Thame to Oxford, and grew a branch to Aylesbury. Much rebuilding was needed to bring it up to main line standards, especially near Saunderton. The Aylesbury branch was also given over to the new joint committee and, like the rest of the Wycombe Railway, had once been broad gauge. Onwards from Princes Risborough, where the station was completely rebuilt, the line was again of new construction and was dead straight for four miles, Hadden-

Below:

Renishaw Central on 2 March 1963, showing a typical Great Central Derbyshire station.

Douglas Thompson

ham being the only station on this section. The Great Western & Great Central Joint line was opened to goods traffic in November 1904, and to passengers in April 1906, which allowed the Great Central a choice of routes out of London. The two companies' lines then diverged at Ashendon Junction, where the Great Central's route swept round to the right, the Great Western's up line flying over the top.

The stations of the Great Central's London extension bore a striking similarity in their spacious and characteristic island platform layout: it had been felt that this provided a more economical means of construction. Typically the platform was reached by stairs down from a road overbridge, or from a subway. Access also had to be provided to at least one side of the layout for carts and lorries. The advantages were offset by a number of problems: one was the need to get certain passenger-rated traffic such as milk (in churns) across at least one of the main running lines on to the platform, and another was the fact that the main lines diverged to pass the platforms, which imposed an increasing restriction as train speeds became higher.

North from Grendon Underwood the main line was relatively easily graded, allowing for the consistently high speeds for which the route was well known, both for passenger and goods traffic. There was a level 'summit' stretch at Charwelton, with troughs on the London side, shortly followed by a long grade down towards Braunston, with Catesby Tunnel near the top. Nottingham Victoria was approached through tunnels in both directions, with two (Mansfield Road and Sherwood Road) on the Sheffield side, and from here on the gradients became more severe. From a maximum of 1 in 176 south of Nottingham the climb started almost immediately at 1 in 130, with about 7 miles of 1 in 130 or 132 past Annesley to the summit just beyond Kirkby South Junction. Having attained the next summit at Pilsley the line then fell through Duckmanton North junction where the loop to Chesterfield diverged, rejoining the main line at Staveley Town; Staveley Works was on the loop. The former was noted for its fine gardens and regularly won special class awards; the Markham colliery branch fed in large quantities of traffic here. Sheffield Victoria was approached on a generally falling gradient from Darnall, although the line rose thence from Woodhouse, which was the

junction for the line through Worksop from Retford, Grimsby and Lincoln. From Woodhouse to Sheffield was quadruple track. An additional complication in this area was the fact that the whole main line between Annesley and Oughtibridge was subject to temporary speed restrictions due to colliery subsidence – but there again, coal provided a very considerable part of the line's income.

After leaving Sheffield, Manchester trains then faced the unremitting grind up to Woodhead, which route was part of the original MS&L line between Manchester and Grimsby, and is undoubtedly best known for its tunnels. Opened late in 1845, the original single track bore was soon joined by another (in 1852), but both were replaced by a double track construction in 1954. The new 3-mile tunnel (which cost £4.25 million) had been authorised by the LNER under powers gained in 1947, and work started in 1948. Services ran to Manchester London Road via Penistone, where the route was joined by the GCR's lines from Wath and Barnsley; additionally the Lancashire & Yorkshire line to Huddersfield, Halifax and Bradford diverged to the west of the station. From Sheffield it was nearly 20 miles of uphill slog at varying gradients, but with five miles of 1 in 120 between Oughtibridge and Thurgoland Tunnel. It was equally hard for an up train from Manchester, which additionally had to cope with the rising grade through Woodhead tunnel.

Electrification of the Woodhead route had been authorised before 1939, but the work that had already started was suspended during the war. Deterioration of the old single line tunnels and their lack of clearance for the overhead equipment led the LNER to decide that a double track replacement was the best option. In conjunction with the new tunnel the route was electrified on the 1,500V DC overhead system, working being brought in by stages. The first was completed in February 1952 when electric locomotives took over the haulage of mineral traffic between Wath, Penistone and Dunford Bridge, and the second in June 1954, when main line passenger and goods trains between Manchester and Penistone went over to electric haulage. The new tunnel was officially opened at 11.0am on 3 June by the Minister of Transport, Mr Lennox-Boyd, with the public opening coming 11 days later. At the same time local trains between Glossop, Hadfield

Left:
LNER 'B1' No 1179 heads a Sheffield-London train near Woodhouse Junction on 28 March 1948.
S. C. Taylor

Above right:
No 27004 stands at Sheffield Victoria on 1 June 1957.
Norman Simmons

Right:
Penistone station in April 1950 with ex-GCR 'C13' No 67434 on a Barnsley train.
Real Photographs K614

and Manchester London Road also went over to electric working, using eight 3-car multiple units with 174 seats. The old Woodhead tunnels were officially abandoned at the same time, on 14 June. The track was not lifted until mid-1957, after which the tunnels were bricked up.

Meanwhile, work had also been in progress elsewhere on the route. Thurgoland tunnel, between Wortley and Penistone, on the line from Sheffield, had been supplemented by a new bore in 1948, the original having one track (the up) repositioned in the centre. Hazlehead Bridge station, west of Penistone, closed to passengers on 6 March 1950, but survived for goods traffic until 1964. Services on the main line between Manchester Central and Penistone were hauled either by Bo+Bo or the new Co-Co electric locomotives, these being changed at Penistone for steam haulage until the third stage of the electrification was completed to Sheffield Victoria, in September 1954. The latter were designed for 90mph running, and seven were built at Gorton Works, starting with No 27000. All of the latter and 14 of the 58 Bo+Bo locomotives were fitted with train-heating boilers, and regenerative braking was also installed. The prototype electric locomotive for the scheme, No 26000, had returned from Holland via Harwich Parkeston Quay early in 1952, where it had been on extensive trials.

The route was extremely heavily graded, the ruling gradient between Wentworth and West Silkstone Junction being 1 in 40. This had necessitated the use of Britain's largest steam locomotive, the LNER's 2-8-0+0-8-2 Beyer Garratt of 1925. 1,100-ton coal trains from Wath to Dunford Bridge were allowed 142min for the 14.25 miles, speeds ranging between 7 and 15mph on the bank from Wentworth, with 86min allowed for express goods trains, which were not less than 50% braked. If the Garratt was not available it was necessary to use four engines, two banking and two hauling. When the change to electric traction was made, one was used at each end of an 850-ton train, giving a speed of about 11-12mph; with the express goods one of them could maintain 22-24mph. Extensive signalling renewal was associated with the electrification scheme. It had originally been envisaged that the old semaphore distant signals would be replaced by electric colour lights, or where signals were likely to be obscured by smoke or steam. However, the Railway Inspectorate recommended the complete replacement of semaphores, and this was done. At the same time several signalboxes were extended: among other things, extra engine movements were needed at the change-over points. The track circuiting arrangements which had hitherto relied on DC circuits had to be altered to AC in order to avoid interference from the traction current return through the rails.

The final stage of the scheme was the electrification to Rotherwood sidings, south of Sheffield, where it was envisaged that all steam-hauled goods trains from the south would change over to electric traction. With the completion of the work, 65 route miles had been converted, with a track mileage of 318, and although the line still had an overall limit of 65mph, the steam timing of 65min for the 41.5 miles between Manchester and Sheffield had been cut to 56min. All freight could now be worked on an 'out and home' basis because of the cuts in transit time, and 50% fewer train crews were needed. Electrification of the Worsborough branch, including the two miles of Wentworth bank at 1 in 40, had removed the problems of attaching and detaching bankers, which had itself greatly contributed to the reduction in train crews. There had also been a reduction in weekend working

on the branch. However, there were problems of braking, and the electric locos were limited to 750 tons on the falling gradients between Woodhead and Manchester; there were also problems with bankers hearing the electro-pneumatic horns of the electric locomotives! In spite of all the changes, no steam sheds had yet been closed by June 1955. In the event, the Woodhead electrification scheme proved to be a great success. In the first three months of electric operation by multiple units, the passenger revenue went up by 123%, and passenger numbers on the Manchester-Sheffield line increased by 43% as a result of the switch to electric haulage. Ironically regional boundary adjustments moved the new Woodhead tunnel into the London Midland Region.

The Beeching closure proposals did not reflect what happened in the end. The report slated the Glossop spur for closure, but otherwise made no mention of the Woodhead route, which was shown as remaining open. The alternative route from Sheffield to Manchester (ie Midland to Central) was to be closed, but the reverse happened: Sheffield Victoria closed in January 1970 along with Dunford Bridge, and the route lasted into the 1980s for freight before being closed and lifted. By contrast, the former Midland line through Chinley, also part of the same London Midland Region, thrives.

Named trains were few on the Great Central lines, being principally the 'Master Cutler' between Marylebone and Sheffield Victoria, and the 'South Yorkshireman' between Marylebone and Bradford Exchange. Both had been introduced after the Second World War, the former on 6 October 1947 and the latter on 31 May 1948. The pattern of express services between Marylebone and Sheffield, Manchester and Bradford in the postwar years had been relatively constant. In 1955 there were five trains in each direction, these being in the down: the 10.0am, 12.15pm and 3.20pm to Sheffield Victoria and Manchester London Road; the 4.40pm (the 'South Yorkshireman') to Sheffield and Bradford

Exchange, and the 6.15pm 'Master Cutler' to Sheffield and Manchester. Additionally there was the 10.0pm train to Manchester, which arrived at 4.2am the following morning and which also conveyed through carriages for Liverpool Central. The 10.0am ran via Harrow-on-the-Hill and called at Aylesbury, Woodford Halse, Rugby Central, Leicester Central, Loughborough Central, Nottingham Victoria and Staveley Central on its way to Sheffield, then stopping at Penistone and Guide Bridge before arriving at Manchester London Road at 3.8pm.

The 'South Yorkshireman' took an hour to reach Aylesbury, its first stop, reaching Leicester Central at 7.3pm. It then called at Nottingham Victoria (7.36pm) and Sheffield Victoria (8.40pm) before again serving Penistone, there leaving the Great Central lines to reach Bradford Exchange at 10.17pm. The 'Master Cutler's' first call was at Rugby Central, then Leicester, Nottingham and Sheffield. On Sundays there were express trains from Marylebone to Sheffield at 12.45am, and at 9.50am and 3.30pm to Manchester, both the latter having restaurant cars. The up weekday workings were at 7.50am (the 'Master Cutler') from Sheffield, the 8.30am restaurant car service from Manchester, the 'South Yorkshireman' at 11.34am from Sheffield (with through coaches from Bradford at 10.0am), and the 1.4 5pm and 4.0pm trains from Manchester. Additionally there was the 12.25am from Sheffield, which started back at Liverpool.

Other long-distance trains used parts of the Great Central's lines. The link between Banbury and Woodford Halse provided an important connection to the Great Western and was much used in the summer for holiday traffic. Even in winter a number of trains were routed that way, such as the 12.4am Sheffield to Swindon, the 10.23am York to Bournemouth West, and the 6.30pm York to Swindon. An innovation in the summer of 1957 was a car-sleeper service from Marylebone to Glasgow St Enoch, which ran on Monday and Wednesday nights.

Local passenger services – in common with other main lines – tended to be rather sparser. At the London end suburban trains worked out as far as Aylesbury, mostly via High Wycombe where many terminated, although some also went through to Princes Risborough. A few terminated at West Ruislip, or started there and went to Risborough or Wycombe. A few of these workings did extend further out and went as far as, say, Brackley. There were some local services from Paddington as well which went mostly via Maidenhead and Bourne End to reach High Wycombe, perhaps terminating there, but probably then going on to serve most of the stations and halts to Aylesbury. This had been the original line, after all.

Further north, stopping services were provided on the main line by a variety of irregular trains. For example, in the winter 1951-2 timetable, there was a 5.40am all stations from Woodford Halse to Leicester Central, which provided a connection into the 6.49am express thence to Manchester, and itself continued as a stopper to Nottingham Victoria, arriving at 7.48am. Another similar all-stations left Woodford Halse at 6.35am, with a Rugby-Leicester stopper only 25min behind it. The 7.40am from Marylebone called at Harrow-on-the-Hill, Northwood and Aylesbury, and then all stations to Leicester, giving some of them, such as Calvert, Helmdon and Culworth their first down train of the day.

Meanwhile there were other trains such as the 6.0am stopper from Nottingham to Sheffield, giving places such as Renishaw Central, Killamarsh Central, Beighton and Woodhouse their first down services; they then saw only another five or so stop in that direction, although many more hurried through. Last trains tended to be fairly early, as on branch lines, and possibly later on Saturdays. The 9.32pm from Marylebone to Brackley Central gave an arrival at 11.47pm, and Belgrave & Birstall, Rothley and Quorn & Woodhouse enjoyed stops on the 9.55pm Leicester to Nottingham, though most others were not so fortunate.

The pattern of local trains did not change significantly through the 1950s, although a few of the smaller stations closed, such as Beighton (November 1954, all services) and Braunston & Willoughby (April 1957, all services). With the final transfer to the London Midland Region in 1959, the inevitable decline set in and services started to thin out, Pilsley station (near Chesterfield) being an early casualty, closing from the start of the winter timetable in November of that year.

The through daytime expresses on the Great Central came off at the very start of 1960, when all daytime through trains between Marylebone and Sheffield, Manchester and Bradford were withdrawn. The 'South Yorkshireman' survived as a named train to the very end, hauled on its very last working by Stanier Class 5 No 45116 as far as Leicester, where Standard Class 5 No 73004 took over; the 'Master Cutler' name had already gone. The York-Bournemouth service, which had loaded reliably, was also terminated at Banbury, with no onward connection being provided! The last day of operation for the expresses was 2 January, after which they were replaced (on Monday 4 January) by three semi-fast services between Marylebone and Nottingham Victoria, running via Aylesbury. They left Nottingham at 8.40am, 12.25pm and 5.15pm, the down services being at 8.40am, 12.40pm (12.25pm Saturdays) and 4.30pm. They also called at Aylesbury, Brackley, Woodford Halse, Rugby Central, Lutterworth, Leicester Central and Loughborough Central. The 'South Yorkshire-

man' was replaced by a train leaving Halifax at 8.30am, Huddersfield at 9.3am, and going forward to Sheffield Midland, where through coaches were attached to the 8.52am from Bradford Forster Square to St Pancras.

The night trains, from Marylebone at 9.55pm Monday to Friday, and Manchester Central at 10.50pm, continued to run. Local services were to be concentrated on the 'Chiltern' area on both routes, but the closure of the smaller stations between Aylesbury and Nottingham was also mooted.

Many people were outraged by these sweeping changes to the Great Central's services. On 9 April 1960 the Great Central Association was formed as a result of a public meeting in Nottingham, with the objective of encouraging the proper use of the Great Central lines by the provision of 'fast, adequate and convenient services'. A charter scheme was under consideration, so that the truth of this might be demonstrated. Ironically however, the 'Master Cutler' name quickly reappeared (on 28 September 1960) on a new locomotive-hauled Pullman train to Sheffield Victoria – but from King's Cross via Retford. The London extension did not linger long, and finally closed to passengers in 1969 north of Aylesbury, having been condemned to death by the Beeching report.

It certainly appeared to many people that the Great Central line was deliberately run down prior to closure. When the express trains came off in 1960 there were bitter accusations that little had been done to publicise the route – on the contrary, British Railways were alleged to have actively discouraged its use. One example was that new diesel services were introduced on the parallel Midland line with much publicity, which attracted many passengers away from the Great Central. Even so, it was said that the local services on the line were safe and that it was to be developed as a fitted freight and parcels artery. The reprieve was short-lived: Aylesbury to Sheffield Victoria local services were put up for closure even before the Beeching report appeared; even the main stations such as Leicester and Loughborough Central became unstaffed in 1966 and finally closed to passengers on 5 May 1969, freight services having gone in 1964.

What of the Great Central's cross-country routes? The Doncaster to Cleethorpes section had been one of the earliest parts of the Manchester, Sheffield & Lincolnshire. It had a relatively sparse passenger service, local stations such as Thorne South, Medge Hall and Crowle seeing no more than one every two or three hours, mostly as calls by the Doncaster-Cleethorpes stoppers. Cleethorpes and Grimsby had a higher level of services, of course, with trains running either via Retford or Scunthorpe to destinations such as Sheffield or Manchester, and there were many dated trains for holiday traffic.

However, the line carried a heavy goods traffic, passing through the heavy industrial areas of south Humberside, and also being on one of the main routes to the railway-owned ports of Immingham and Grimsby. Travelling eastwards from Doncaster,

Above right:

Looking along platform 4 at Victoria, inside the train shed. There is a wealth of detail in this view taken on 18 September 1964: Dr Beeching proposed it for closure, and it lasted only three more years.
Douglas Thompson

Right:

A splendid 1964 view of the booking office at Nottingham Victoria, with many obviously modern items such as the cigarette vending machines and the litter bins, but fully retaining the elegance given by its builders at the turn of the century.
Douglas Thompson

the first station was Barnby Dun, whose main traffic derived from its private sidings. Pilkington's glass was the largest of these, and produced a variety of finished products such as plate glass and bottles, which in 1961 amounted to 12,640 tons for the home market and 6,620 tons for export, with a further 6,300 tons of bottles. Rockware Glass also used the siding. Inward traffic here amounted to 82,000 tons of sand, 24,000 tons of soda ash and 64,000 tons of coal in the same year. Another customer was the maltsters G. F. Milnthorp Ltd, forwarding 321 tons of malt in 1961 and receiving 1,046 tons of barley and 454 tons of coal. Another short-term traffic was construction material for the new power station at Thorp Marsh, which necessitated the delivery of some 19,000 tons of steelwork. Considerable tonnages of potatoes were also forwarded.

At the next station, Stainforth & Hatfield, there was a large yard mainly for the steel traffic from Frodingham. There were 70 goods trains booked to call each day, with 120 wagonloads of coal daily from Hatfield Colliery: in all, the yards handled around 4,500 wagons per week. Thorne South had a heavy inward coal traffic, and also steel for the shipyards; less conventionally it also acted as a forwarding point for produce from Borstal farms,

which was sent to prisons around the country. Additionally, a local greyhound breeder despatched animals by rail to various tracks.

Crowle, on the other hand, only 16 miles from Doncaster, was primarily concerned with agricultural traffic such as potatoes and sugar beet, and also operated a parcels delivery service within a radius of ten miles. Additionally, it was a 'cattle-truck cleaning station', which must have been one of the less sought-after jobs on the railway. The stationmaster at Crowle was also in charge of Medge Hall after it closed to passengers in September 1960, where a moss peat works daily produced about 20 tons of bales and turfs. Because of the nature of the land here – much of it had been extensively drained by a network of dikes – it was extremely popular with anglers, and special trains were run to Crowle on Sundays in the fishing season.

Further along the line at Althorpe the stationmaster was also in charge of Keadby goods yard, jetty and power station, and also Gunness goods yard. The railway crossed the River Trent by Keadby lifting bridge, the goods station being on a spur. The main line looped to the south to cross the river, Althorpe station being on the west bank and Gunness goods on the east, with

Gunhouse Wharf facing Keadby goods on the opposite bank. At the latter, sugar beet and potatoes were loaded; 20,000 tons of coal per week went to the power works, and oil was also shipped there. Coal was also loaded directly into ships from rail wagons by means of an electrically-operated winch and chute on the jetty. Gunness goods dealt with potatoes and agricultural implements, whilst Althorpe itself was passenger-only.

Scunthorpe & Frodingham handled a huge amount of traffic, the majority associated with the steel industry. The biggest user was the United Steel Companies Ltd; associated works included the Thomas Whitehead Bar & Strip Co Ltd, several companies dealing in slag, mining companies, concrete companies, the East Midlands Gas Board and Wagon Repairs Ltd. In 1961 Scunthorpe issued 103,829 passenger tickets and collected a further 170,446. Parcels traffic was also very large, helped at the end of the 1950s and early 1960s by the attraction to rail of cut flowers, sent away in boxes.

Appleby and Elsham also shared a stationmaster, although nearly five miles apart. At Appleby much of the traffic was agricultural, but Elsham loaded up to 60 wagonloads of lime and limestone each week for the steel works at Scunthorpe. Barnetby and Brocklesby also shared a stationmaster. Barnetby, being the junction of the former Great Central lines to Lincoln, Retford, Doncaster and Cleethorpes, boasted the second-largest manual signalbox in the country in 1961, and handled considerable amounts of goods traffic, including 100,000 tons of limestone annually. Habrough was principally a passenger station; Stallingborough, Healing and Great Coates all came under a single stationmaster, and between them issued around 80,000 passenger tickets annually, with a further 220,000 being collected.

Grimsby Town and Docks stations, New Clee and Cleethorpes also came under the aegis of one stationmaster. Passenger traffic was considerable, and the more so in the summer, with Cleethorpes seeing up to 90 trains a day in the peak summer period. Far more tickets were collected than issued: for example, at Grimsby Town the figures were respectively 537,000 and 272,000, and at Cleethorpes 370,893 and 73,902. The freight traffic through the docks was very varied but included, curiously, up to 1,600 tons of fish arriving by rail, mostly salmon from Scotland. More conventionally, Grimsby despatched 80,000cwt of fish in Easter week alone in 1949. Grimsby was also a pioneer of frozen food traffic which grew very rapidly in the 1950s and 60s.

Much of the former Great Central is now closed, certainly to passengers, although most of the Lincolnshire parts survive – Cleethorpes, Grimsby, Immingham and their lines westwards. They still see direct services to Sheffield and Manchester, but not to Victoria and certainly not via Woodhead. The London extension is long gone although occasional 'specials' still run to Quainton Road, and waste goes to Calvert. Paradoxically Marylebone, under threat for so long, enjoys a renaissance as the terminus of the 'Chiltern Line' services and even sports direct trains to Birmingham Snow Hill. Who would have thought it!

CHAPTER 8
Great Central Motive Power

Great Central locomotives generally survived quite well through the grouping era and into British Railways days, about 600 still being in service in 1960, scattered among the Eastern, North Eastern, Scottish and London Midland Regions. They were as follows: 38 Class A5 4-6-2Ts, introduced in 1911 and built by both the Great Central and the LNER, with many still in service on trains shortly to be replaced by railcars; 35 of the famous 'Director' Class D11 4-4-0; 11 'C13/C14' 4-4-2 tanks; 28 Class J10 0-6-0s and no fewer than 115 of the 'Pom-poms' – the 'J11' 0-6-0s. These were popular engines, built for freight but sometimes used on passenger turns when the pressure was on. Some had been modified with long-travel pistons and a raised boilerline. There were 40 'N5' 0-6-2 tanks and a combined total of 324 Class O1/O4 2-8-0s, which had originally been introduced by Robinson in 1911, the 'O1s' being a rebuild by Thompson with a round-topped firebox. Finally there were still 9 Class Q1 tanks in service, themselves rebuilds from 'Q4s'.

All of the ex-GCR 4-6-0s were withdrawn by 1960, 90 (in 9 classes) having been taken over by LNER in 1923, with 10 more Class B7s being built by the LNER in 1923/4. The *Lord Faringdon* ('B3') class had been express passenger engines, but had been heavy on coal, and the last was scrapped in 1949. The 'B7s' had

been a smaller-wheeled version of the 'B3s', and were used on fast freight work. Members of Class B2 had also been named, the first being *Sir Sam Fay*, others being named after cities served by the Great Central, including Lincoln, Manchester, Chester, London and Liverpool. They were two-cylinder engines with 6ft 9in drivers, and in common with GCR practice there was also a smaller-wheeled version, with 5ft 7in drivers. Four out of eleven of the latter had been named, including No 5004 *Glenalmond* which was the last of its class and worked out its days soon after the end of the war on stopping trains between Marylebone and Leicester. The only other named 4-6-0 on the Great Central had been 'B4' No 6097 *Immingham*, which was withdrawn from service in November 1950, the other 4-6-0s following very shortly afterwards.

Of the 146 GCR 4-4-0s taken over at the Grouping only 11 were left in service by 1960, plus 24 that had been built by the LNER in 19 24, and all of the survivors were members of Class

Below:
A light load for 'B1' No 61206 on the 12.0 noon Leicester-Woodford Halse leaving Ashby Magna on 2 December 1961.
M. Mitchell

Above:
Much 'rationalisation' is unfortunately evident as 'V2' No 60886 heads a southbound goods near Charwelton on 13 February 1965.
Gerald T. Robinson

Left:
A four-car diesel multiple unit attracts plenty of business at Lutterworth in July 1965, although the weather looks less than summery. Sadly, the station is looking rather run-down.
Andrew Muckley

Right:
Standard '9F' No 92092 prepares for the climb up Ashby Magna bank as it approaches Whetstone with an up Annesley-Woodford Halse 'runner'. Fast freight trains such as these were a feature of the Great Central main line for many years, and were often known as 'Windcutters'.
Colin P. Walker

Below right:
Class B1 No 61108 heads the down 12.15pm from Marylebone to Manchester near Denham on the Great Western & Great Central Joint line in April 1950.
Locomotive Publishing Co 24750

Below:
Class A5 4-6-2 No 69821 heads an up suburban service, partly composed of articulated stock, through Harefield in February 1950.
Locomotive Publishing Co 23597

D11, the 'Directors'. The 1913 design had been modified to fit the Scottish loading gauge, and all of this later batch worked north of the border. All of the originals bore the names of GCR directors, hence the name of the class. The 'Directors' were the last surviving Great Central passenger engines, but by 1960 many were in store: Nos 62660, 62662, 62664, and 62666-70 at Darnall (41A), with Nos 62661/3 at Staveley (41H).

The *Sir Sam Fay* and *Immingham* 4-6-0s had been seen relatively rarely in the London area, mostly working from Sheffield, Immingham or Leeds. They did sometimes appear in the south in the summer, when they might be seen working the 'Norway Cruise' boat trains between Marylebone and Immingham Docks. Although introduced for fast express work, the 'Directors' had long been replaced on the London extension by the 'Sandringhams' and later the (then) 'A1' Pacifics, subsequently 'A3s'. These were in turn replaced by 'V2s' towards the end of 1957, whilst the 'Directors' had largely survived on secondary passenger duties in Cheshire and Lincolnshire. The Great Central continued to receive new locomotives almost until the end, however, with No 80144 going to Neasden in 1956, BR Standard 2-10-0s Nos 92094/5 to Annesley in May 1957, and No 92191 to Darnall as late as August 1958.

Although the London end of the Great Central line had been allocated to the Western Region (on geographical grounds) soon after nationalisation, its services continued to be operated by the Eastern – hence the essentially LNER appearance of its trains. However, in 1958 the whole was transferred to the London Midland, and this brought about considerable change: the 'V2s' were replaced by Stanier 'Black 5s', the LNER 'L1s' were replaced by Ivatt 2-6-4 tanks and the elderly Robinson 4-4-2 tanks on the Chesham branch by Ivatt 2-6-2 tanks. Freight saw a brief appearance of the Standard 2-10-0s, and passenger stock saw the appearance of standard BR and ex-LMS coaches. The last named trains were in the hands of ex-LMS or BR standard engines.

The Great Central section had also hosted the 1,500V DC Woodhead electrification scheme, and locomotives and multiple-unit stock were required. The trains for the Manchester suburban services consisted of eight 3-car sets comprising a motor coach, trailer and driving trailer and having first and third class seating for 174 passengers. There were four motors in each motor coach with electro-pneumatic contactor control, each being rated at 185hp full field and 210hp weak field. The coach bodies were similar to those of the Liverpool Street-Shenfield stock, with two pairs of electro-pneumatic sliding doors and permissive passenger control. The interiors were finished with varnished birch- and sycamore-veneered plywood, with ceilings and spandrels painted cream. The large windows were teak framed and the seats finished in blue moquette in the smokers' sections, and russet elsewhere. The metal screens by the door ways were fitted with 0.375in armour-plate glass panels.

The new Co-Co locomotives had a 90mph maximum, with buffing and drawgear on the body, rather than on the bogies as on the earlier Bo+Bo classes. The cabs had a side-corridor connection, but the doors giving access to high-tension and resistance chambers were interlocked with the master controller, so that access was possible only when the power was off and the pantograph down. Their length over buffers was 59ft 0in and wheelbase 46ft 2in, and they weighed 102 tons. The electrical equipment was supplied by Metropolitan-Vickers; they had three nose-suspended motors in each bogie, again with control by electro-pneumatic contactors. Roller-bearing axleboxes and regenerative braking was fitted, as on the Bo+Bos. No 27000 was the first of the series of Co-Cos.

Below:
Stoke Mandeville station, just short of Aylesbury on the Metropolitan & Great Central Joint line, clearly shows evidence of its ownership and operation by London Transport, even though it has all the attributes of a country station – the gardens, the ancient lower-quadrant signal, the water-butt and so on. British Railways did not take it over until the early 1960s.
Lens of Sutton

Right:
Chesham was the terminus of the short branch from Chalfont & Latimer, and although on the joint line was operated by the Great Central. The goods yard was beyond the platform, behind the camera.
Lens of Sutton

Below right:
An almost timeless view of a down Aylesbury train on 3 June 1939, headed by 'A5' No 5452, near Chorley Wood.
Locomotive Publishing Co 65535

Below:
Marylebone station seen from its approaches in 1953. Of all the London termini it was characterised by an unhurried elegance, and its quietness and period flavour has endeared it to film makers over the years.
Locomotive & General 27336

The Great Eastern Lines

The Great Eastern area of the Eastern Region had remained almost unchanged in extent since that company was formed back in 1862. The two main lines ran into Liverpool Street, with a network of connecting branches ramifying throughout East Anglia. Of course there had been changes: Liverpool Street opened in 1874, and was greatly enlarged in the 1890s; quadrupling had taken place out to Shenfield in the 1930s, and the LNER had effectively taken over the Midland & Great Northern system in 1936, when Great Eastern locomotives finally managed to infiltrate the territory of their only serious local rival. The LNER had also swallowed up the tiny and impecunious Mid-Suffolk Light Railway at the grouping in 1923, together with the Colne Valley line, leaving the narrow gauge Southwold Railway as an intruder, which closed in 1929. Finally, with nationalisation, the London, Tilbury & Southend line came into the fold, having been snatched by the Midland back in 1912.

East Anglia is known, of course, for being flat, which it isn't! True fenland does have the almost eerie quality of complete flatness, perhaps best reflected in the lines radiating from Ely. However, it is far more accurate to describe the terrain as 'rolling', and so the many secondary lines and branches, most built at minimal cost, tended to be a bit like roller-coasters, and there were some fearsome banks. The East Suffolk line, from

Ipswich to Yarmouth, was a good example, with Westerfield providing a stiff challenge to crews and engines lifting a heavy express away from the speed restriction at East Suffolk junction. The main line to Norwich presented a number of challenges such as Belstead bank south of Ipswich, to say nothing of the self-imposed climb out of Norwich to cross Lakenham viaduct, taking the Ipswich line over that to Thetford and Ely.

The main routes went north-south, with the east-west flows being somewhat secondary. Holiday traffic arriving from the Midlands to the holiday resorts on the east coast – Yarmouth, Lowestoft, Cromer, Sheringham and Clacton could either travel via the Great Eastern's lines, or (for the first four at least) via the Midland & Great Northern. There had been many challenges to the Great Eastern's monopoly, and to that of its predecessor, the Eastern Counties Railway, but few ultimately succeeded, and the only line of note that came into being was the Eastern & Midland. When the opportunity arose, the Midland and Great North-

Below:

Liverpool Street station, home of the Great Eastern in London, with No 69725 ready to leave at 9.15am. The platform is full of trolleys and barrows stacked with parcels and packets.
David Lawrence

ern companies took the chance to grab a share of the new holiday markets in Norfolk and Suffolk by taking over the E&M, and they made determined efforts to drum up traffic and route it via their new line. It was difficult and expensive to work, with extensive single track sections and a number of difficult banks, and in 1936 the LNER took it over completely. Operations continued in much the same way as before, and it was closed almost in its entirety in 1959 – one of the first major closures in the country. However, it carried a great deal of holiday traffic on summer Saturdays, and quantities of agricultural traffic, and fish.

The Eastern Region inherited all of these lines – the intensive London suburban services, the remote branch lines, the long-distance main lines and the cross-country secondary routes. With them came an assortment of motive power, some elderly in the extreme, and some more modern. It had always been low on the priority list for new locomotives and stock, and although it had some reasonable expresses (such as the 'East Anglian' to Norwich), they suffered the same restrictions of tractive effort as other services. Lack of any heavy industry or mineral resources had always restricted investment in the area's railways, but before too long it was to come to the forefront.

In 1949 the first phase of the suburban electrification programme came to fruition, when the power was turned on for the Liverpool Street to Shenfield service. The wires spread progressively outwards to Chelmsford and Southend, and then on to Colchester and Clacton, and all before Dr Beeching's time. Other schemes sparked the suburban lines to Hertford East, Chingford and the Lea Valley, and saw the reopening of the abandoned Churchbury loop. Other major projects included the flyovers at Shenfield and Ilford, and the rebuilding of Chelmsford and Colchester stations.

The two main lines were those via Ipswich to Norwich and via Cambridge to King's Lynn. The former had been regarded by the Great Eastern as extending to Cromer, and the Wensum curve allowed expresses to avoid Norwich Thorpe station. Services operated via Ipswich to Cromer and Sheringham and to Yarmouth South Town over the East Suffolk line. Through coaches arrived from a wide variety of other destinations, and once it had been the intention to run crack expresses to Wells, with a high-speed link being built on to that branch from Forncett to Wymondham.

There were six tracks out of Liverpool Street as far as Bethnal Green, whence four went towards Cambridge and four towards Norwich. On the latter route Stratford was another major junction, with the works and the loco sheds occupying a huge area between the Norwich line and the old Cambridge line. The station had been completely reconstructed just before the war to accommodate the Central Line of the London Underground which briefly emerged into the daylight there, although it didn't actually arrive until after hostilities had ceased. A string of suburban stations followed, all variously rebuilt in the 1930s with the widening, on through Brentwood and its notorious bank to Shenfield, where the line to Southend Victoria diverged. This was a relative newcomer, not being opened until 1 October 1889; the line from Shenfield to Wickford had opened in November of the previous year.

The line was carried to Chelmsford over a long viaduct, and together with the station was on a tight curve, necessitating a severe speed restriction, still in force today. The line onward was a difficult one to build and maintain, since the Essex clay saw to it that the roadbed was unstable and liable to subsidence. Double junctions at Witham saw the Maldon and Braintree branches diverge, with the idiosyncratic Kelvedon & Tollesbury Light railway soon after. Marks Tey was a different matter since the Stour Valley and Colne Valley lines trailed in on the down side, between

Above right:
In September 1960 'L1' No 67727 arrives bunker-first (as was the custom) at Liverpool Street with a suburban service from Bishop's Stortford. No 69742 is also in view. Note the Westinghouse pumps on all the Great Eastern section suburban locomotives.
John C Baker

Right:
The Great Eastern ran suburban services to an intensity quite unmatched by any other LNER constituent, with a dense network of lines equalled only by the Southern. Here, 'N7' No 69640 is seen arriving at Custom House with the 3.30pm North Woolwich to Stratford on 7th September 1961.
D. E. Esau

Below:
A typical Great Eastern suburban shed, where most of the work was done for the suburban services. Here Walthamstow Wood Street is seen in October 1955; venerable 'N7' No 69604 is in residence.
Real Photographs K2807

them providing an important cross-country link between Cambridge and the north Essex ports of Colchester and Harwich, and later the holiday traffic to Clacton and Walton.

Colchester itself – always an important town – had its station inconveniently situated to the north, and had been the subject of much acrimonious wrangling in the early days of the railways. Again subject to severe speed restrictions because of the curvature of the line (but this time for no obvious reason), it remains an important junction for Clacton and Walton, and once for Brightlingsea. The line continued northwards to Manningtree, again a junction for Harwich, and having crossed the Stour estuary into Suffolk, forged on to Ipswich. This town also has a complex railway history and remains an important junction, this time for the East Suffolk line, the Felixstowe branch, and its docks branches. The line from Colchester had been built by a different company, the Eastern Union, and its rivalry with the Eastern Counties explains many of the apparent oddities of railway geography in the area. The main line was built to Bury St Edmunds, with the extension from Haughley Junction to Norwich somewhat of an afterthought, but built very much as a main line, for speed.

By the time British Railways had emerged on the scene, the Eye and Hadleigh branches had long been reduced to goods-only status. Dreams of express trains to Wells had long gone, and Norwich Victoria had been reduced to the status of a goods station. Norwich Thorpe, of course, was the hub of the city's railways, with lines coming in from Yarmouth Vauxhall, Lowestoft, Cromer and Ely; trains also arrived from Wells, King's Lynn and Beccles via the Waveney Valley. The swing bridges of Norfolk and Suffolk provided a characteristic railway feature of an area where lines often had to cross navigable waterways, especially when traversing the marshes.

The line from Norwich to Ely, on the other hand, struck out across the brecks of Norfolk – heathland or woodland of very different character. The Wells line went through Dereham – an important junction with no less than four signalboxes, and also to King's Lynn, with local stations having characteristic buildings of flint which left the traveller in no doubt as to location. The M&GN served essentially the same places, also wandering across country from Yarmouth Beach through the broads (much of it now converted into a main road), through Melton Constable where the lines to Norwich and Cromer joined, and on to South Lynn. Much has been written about Melton Constable, that microcosm of a Midlands industrial town transplanted into the Norfolk countryside; the visitor today can still conjure up the ghosts of the past with its terraced houses and the remains of the works. By the time the Eastern Region came into being it had lost much of its importance: the works had closed when the LNER took over, and it was no more than a place where some smart train working took place on summer Saturdays.

The King's Lynn line diverged from the Norwich at Bethnal Green, and made a tortuous exit from the capital via Hackney Downs. Running down the Lea valley, the Churchbury loop rejoined at Cheshunt; then on to Broxbourne, which was rebuilt in connection with the electrification to Bishop's Stortford and Hertford, completed in November 1960. A mile beyond the station the branch to Hertford East diverged, the former providing a rail connection to the Great Northern, although this did not survive the 1960s. St Margarets, on the Hertford line, was the junction for the branch to Buntingford, nearly 14 miles away. This still retained through services to Liverpool Street in the morning and evening peaks in the 1950s, but succumbed to the inevitable road competition and closed to passengers on 16 November 1964, lingering for goods until September of the following year.

The main line, following the Essex-Hertfordshire border crossed into the former to pass through Roydon, Burnt Mill and Harlow. Harlow had been designated as the site of one of the postwar 'new towns', and its population mushroomed. Burnt Mill was duly rebuilt and renamed Harlow Town, and the former Harlow had 'Mill' suffixed to it. Having passed Sawbridgeworth the line soon reached Bishop's Stortford, having crossed back into Hertfordshire. Always a busy station it was also the junction for the line which wandered across from Witham, through Braintree. It carried a decidedly infrequent service – in winter 1951 it saw seven trains each way on weekdays, one less on Saturdays; probably its best-known traffic was the bacon flitches from Dunmow. It was an early casualty, losing its passenger service in March 1952, although it survived for goods until 1969.

The main line then continued northwards through Essex via Stansted, at the foot of the short but fierce bank to Elsenham, the summit of the line. Here was the junction for the short-lived Elsenham & Thaxted light railway, which lasted a mere 50 years, closing in 1953. The main line dropped down through Newport and Audley End, which was followed closely by two tunnels

Right:

Out on the main line Pacific No 70040 *Clive of India* storms past Witham with the up 'East Anglian' in May 1956.

Locomotive Publishing Co 23402

(Audley End and Littlebury), each around a quarter mile long. At Audley End station the branch to Saffron Walden joined, providing a connection also to the Cambridge-Colchester line at Bartlow. Saffron Walden, like so many towns, had been missed by the main lines when they were built, and although its branch arrived in 1865 and arrested its slow decline, it did not grow to any great size. In spite of efforts at revival, including the building of Acrow halt (by a local engineering company) in 1957, it closed to passengers on 7 September 1964.

Once having cleared the Lea Valley, Bishop's Stortford and their many restrictions, expresses were able finally to show a turn of speed before getting to Cambridge. The line not only saw trains to King's Lynn and Hunstanton, but also a service of expresses to Norwich via Thetford, and it is only in relatively recent years that the supremacy of the Ipswich route finally became established. In the 1951 timetable, for instance, there were five trains to Norwich via Cambridge, four of which carried either a restaurant or buffet car, and taking about 3hr 30min for the journey; at the same time the Ipswich line was showing 2hr 10min for the fastest trains to Norwich (the Cromer expresses,

calling en route at Ipswich only). The Cambridge line also served a variety of other destinations: the 'Fenman' served King's Lynn, but carried through coaches for Bury St Edmunds, detached or attached at Cambridge, and other through trains went to March and Wisbech via Ely.

The main line to King's Lynn, now electrified and extensively singled, really is a stereotypical East Anglian line. It runs almost straight across the fens, all but level all the way, and with fields of carrots, onions and potatoes on either side growing in the rich peat soil. King's Lynn was a terminal station, and trains continuing on to Hunstanton had to reverse there, no avoiding line being provided. As with Norwich, it was also a junction for several other lines, in this case those to South Lynn (on the M&GN) and Dereham. There was also an extensive system serving the docks.

CHAPTER 10 Great Eastern Services

The railways out of Liverpool Street carried a considerable variety of services, and the London terminus has always been noted for the intensity of its suburban workings. The Great Eastern ran a suburban service of great intensity at very tight headways, using diminutive steam locomotives, and which necessitated the use of the Westinghouse system in order to give the braking characteristics demanded for the rapid station stops. This was retained by the LNER, even though it made the vacuum brake standard elsewhere after the 1923 grouping. Electrification was considered in the years preceding World War 2, but was postponed through lack of finance and the outbreak of hostilities. The first part was finally implemented on 9 November 1949, when the resignalling of Liverpool Street was finished; the regular-interval electric service to Gidea Park and Shenfield had been introduced on 26 September. The opening ceremony had been performed by Alfred Barnes, the Minister of Transport, who first cut the ceremonial ribbon across one of the entries of a new sliding-door electric set (later designated Class 306) and then drove the unit.

The electrification system adopted at this time was 1,500V DC overhead, later converted to 25kV AC, with parts using 6.25kV where clearances could not easily be obtained for the higher voltage. Subsequently the whole system was converted to the 25kV standard, partly in the light of the experience gained with the experimental work on the Clacton and Walton lines. The new electric trains were an immediate success, and with tight diagram-ming and good passenger loadings became among the most profitable on the Eastern Region. The off-peak service pattern for the electrics was to run all-stations from Liverpool Street to Gidea Park at 10, 30 and 50 minutes past each hour, with Shenfield trains (calling at Stratford, Ilford, Romford, then all stations) at 5, 25 and 45 minutes past the hour. This varied in the peaks, of course, and between 5.0pm and 5.59pm in the winter

Below:
Mistley station, on the Harwich branch, basks in the summer sunshine, although its gardens look overgrown and uncared-for.
Lens of Sutton

Right:
A bleak February day in 1955 at Wickford, with 'B12' No 61557 arriving with a Southend train. The electrification scheme commenced shortly afterwards.
Real Photographs K2458

Below right:
On 6 September 1952 an up Yarmouth to Liverpool Street express, headed by 'B12' No 61542, crosses the River Waveney by Beccles Swing Bridge. Built in 1927, together with the similar one at St Olaves, they were both the most modern in the area and also the first to close, lasting only just over 30 years.
R. E. Vincent

1951 timetable there were 18 electric departures scheduled from Liverpool Street.

In 1955 a £2.5 million scheme to electrify the lines from Shenfield to Chelmsford and Southend Victoria was inaugurated. The 9.75-mile section on the main line saw the opening ceremonies on Friday 8 June 1956, with a special train from Chelmsford to Shenfield and back. The new scheme reached Southend at the end of the year, the inaugural train running on 28 December and public services starting on 31 December. Both of the new sections used the existing 1,500V DC system, though it was intended that they be converted to 25kV AC at a later date. In 1958 the Liverpool Street area saw 73 million originating passenger journeys, equivalent to 121 people per minute; this needed three trains every four minutes, or sixty trains per hour in the peaks. It gener-

ated £7.75m in revenue in that year. By March 1960 the Liverpool Street traffic area still needed a staff of over 10,000, and although the local Clacton scheme had been completed, the lines to Southend and Chelmsford were still at 1,500V DC. There were 268 steam and 130 diesel locomotives, one-third of the passenger service being operated by diesel power. In October of that year the Chelmsford-Shenfield service reverted to steam or diesel operation whilst the overhead line was converted for 25kV AC traction, and the Southend-Shenfield-Liverpool Street route was changed to 6.25kV AC over the weekend of 4-6 November. When the 1955 modernisation plan was announced it was expected that the electrification would be extended to include Ipswich, Clacton, and the Harwich and Felixstowe branches. Whilst it didn't take too long to get to Chelmsford or even Clacton, Ipswich was not finally reached until 1985 and Harwich in 1986; Felixstowe is yet to come, although freight for the docks is now electrically-hauled to Ipswich.

The electrification to Chelmsford extended 22 trains daily from Shenfield, thus providing through services with Ilford, Romford and so on. The pattern of off-peak electric trains from Liverpool Street now looked something like this:

Every 20 minutes – all stations to Gidea Park
Hourly to Stratford, Ilford, Romford and all stations to Chelmsford
Hourly to Shenfield and stations to Southend
Twice an hour to Stratford, Ilford, Romford and all stations to Southend

There were various peak hour extras, and certain stations continued to be served by longer distance steam trains, such as some of the express services to Norwich and beyond which called at Chelmsford. The Clacton interval expresses called at Shenfield and Chelmsford, thus providing the former with one of its few refreshment car services. This facility had begun with the summer timetable for 1950, when regular hourly expresses had started running throughout the day, each conveying a buffet car and taking between 106 and 126min for the journey. Prior to this, in the summer 1946 timetable for example, the first through train to London from Walton (and Frinton and Kirby Cross) and Clacton was at 7.53am and 8.0am respectively, the portions combining at Thorpe-le-Soken, and conveying a buffet car from Walton; it arrived at Liverpool Street at 9.41am, having called intermediately only at Chelmsford. The next was at 9.8am from Clacton, and called at all stations, including St Botolphs, to Colchester North, and taking over three hours for the journey: and that was it for the through service to London!

The interval service revolutionised matters, and even though the trains ran only about every three hours in the winter timetable, that was a vast improvement on what had gone before. In the 1955-6 timetable there were seven through trains in each direction on week days, and two more on Saturdays, though these did not all convey buffet cars; certainly the 11.15pm from Liverpool Street did not. The best time was 103min by the 7.40am up from Clacton. By the summer of 1959 the Britannias had revolutionised the timings, being introduced on to the interval service at the start of the year. The down 'Essex Coast Express', leaving Liverpool Street at 5.27pm , arrived at Clacton only 86min later, calling at Colchester (6.24pm) and Thorpe-le-Soken (6.44pm) only. A connecting stopping train left Colchester at 6.29pm, arriving at Clacton at 7.1pm; this was closely followed by another interval service, the 5.40pm from London, which reached Clacton at 7.17pm. There were thirteen interval expresses in that weekday timetable, all conveying a buffet car except the 6.53 and 7.59pm up from Clacton. Incidentally, while steam still reigned on the Clacton and Walton express and local services, diesel multiple units had taken over the Brightlingsea trains, generally starting either from Wivenhoe or St Botolphs.

Harwich and Parkeston Quay provided another source of traffic. In summer 1946, with the continental routes recovering after the war, the boat trains were running again, the 'Hook Continental' having been reinstated in November 1945, but on a restricted basis. By 1951, timings had improved somewhat, with the train now leaving Liverpool Street at 8.0pm (7.30pm before 8 October) and running daily, its time cut to 90min; the balancing working left Parkeston daily at 7.15am. In 1946 the 'Scandinavian' left London at 3.55pm on Wednesdays and Saturdays, and took 105min for the journey; there was no corresponding train in the other direction. Otherwise, travellers for the branch had to change at Manningtree, except for the one through service from Peterborough North, which left there at 3.58pm and arrived at Harwich Town at 7.53pm; the return working left at 1.0pm.

Ipswich was the destination for a number of stopping trains from the south. Some services ran through from Liverpool Street and called at almost all stations: the 6.50am in the 1946 timetable was one such, finally arriving at 9.43am. There were faster ways to travel, of course, and the 8.12pm Norwich express arrived at Ipswich only twenty minutes behind it. In this way, the smaller stations such as Ardleigh and Bentley were served, and given connections for onward travel. As the years progressed, the need for feats of endurance such as the 6.50 were lessened, and such trains had many of the stops at the London end cut out. Local services then tended to run between Colchester and Ipswich, but at irregular intervals and with many variations. For instance, the celebrated Colchester-York train, which left at 5.15pm in the winter 1951 timetable, covered the local stops to Ipswich and then called at Stowmarket, Bury and Ely.

Trains radiated from Ipswich in all directions. Quite apart from the Norwich line, services left for the East Suffolk – often through coaches detached from a Norwich train – the Felixstowe branch, and the Ely and Cambridge routes. With a considerable concentration of freight traffic to add to things, it was a bustling place indeed. In 1951, the 1.30pm from Liverpool Street would arrive on Platform 3 at 3.11pm, and the rear portion would be detached. The front portion, with the buffet car, would be worked forward to Cromer, calling at Stowmarket, Finningham, Mellis, Diss, Burston (Saturdays only), Tivetshall and Norwich, whilst the rear was taken forward at 3.24pm for principal stations to Yarmouth South Town. This particular train also connected at Stowmarket for Bury. By the summer of 1957 the division of trains had largely finished at Ipswich, the practice increasingly being to provide connecting services. Clearly this was not possible with the 'Easterling', which left Liverpool Street at 11.3am, with a 'Britannia' and nine coaches, and whose first and only stop en route to Yarmouth South Town was Beccles, where the Lowestoft portion was detached. It was most unusual to run through Ipswich: the 8.20am Norwich, 9.30am Sheringham, 12.30pm Melton Constable, 3.30pm Sheringham, 3.33pm Yarmouth South Town and 6.30pm Norwich all made it their first stop, with many others calling there after Chelmsford or Colchester.

With the advent of the 'Britannias' the 1951 express timetable had been converted to departures at half-past the hour, and they were at 10.30am, 12.30pm, 1.30pm and 3.30pm to Cromer, the latter being the 'Broadsman'. As with the 'Norfolkman', this went to Holt and Cromer High, with the train dividing at North Walsham. The 4.30pm was a Norwich train, and the 5.30pm a Cromer; the 7.30pm also terminated at Norwich. Between these, at 6.30pm, was the 'East Anglian', which had its beginning on 27 September 1937, when it was introduced to give a service on Mondays to Fridays between London and Norwich at an average speed of over 51mph. It was suspended for 7 years because of the war, being reintroduced on 7 October 1946, using the same six coaches that had been specially designed by Gresley, and which had attracted so much interest when they first appeared. It was also seen as a train for businessmen, the up departure being at 11.45am from Norwich. Morning meetings in Ipswich or Norwich could be followed by a meal on the train, afternoon meetings in the capital, and an evening meal on the return journey.

In the up direction, the service from Norwich had been similarly rearranged, with the 'Broadsman' at 7.45am, Cromers at 8.45 and 9.45am, the 'East Anglian' at 11.45am, a Melton Constable at 1.45pm, Norwich at 2.45 and 3.45pm, Cromer at

Above:
On 23 August 1958 'J15' No 45466 arrives at Bartlow with a train from Cambridge; the fireman prepares to collect the tablet for the single line section to Haverhill ahead.
Hugh Davies

Left:
The former Great Eastern line between Bartlow and Audley End was served by a variety of motive power over the years, including the ex-North Eastern 'G5s'. In August 1953 No 67322 is seen approaching Saffron Walden from Bartlow.
Locomotive Publishing Co 24738

Right:
A striking portrait of 'B17' No 61642 *Kilverstone Hall* on a down Norwich express at Broxbourne in July 1955. The area was renowned for the large number of glasshouses.
Locomotive Publishing Co 25337

4.45pm, the 'Norfolkman' at 5.45pm (arriving in London at 7.55pm) and a Cromer at 6.45pm. The trains were now both heavier and faster, the fastest trains carrying nine or ten coaches instead of eight, and taking exactly two hours for the journey. On the other hand the 7.23pm all-stations to Ipswich connected there for London, now arrived as early as 12.7am!

The beginning of the end for main line steam came in 1958, when the 2,000hp Type 4 diesel electric locomotives began to be delivered by English Electric; they became better known in recent years as the Class 40s. The first of them, D200, made its demonstration run from Liverpool Street to Norwich on 18 April 1958 in the capable hands of Driver G. S. Marle, the train also carrying H. C. Johnson, Eastern Region General Manager at the time. Ten of the new locomotives were allocated to the Eastern Region, and they were to be used on a proportion of the main Norwich trains, thus allowing the 'Britannias' to be released for the Clacton service. One interesting feature of the new engines was that they had a water tank capacity of 800gal, and that they had a water pick-up fitted: steam heating of coaches was still the order of the day. Making tea on the footplate was rather a different matter compared with a steamer, and with night running it was easy enough to accidentally switch off the engine lamps when brewing up! In steam days, a driver could be pulled up by a signalman and told that he had 'both eyes shut' – the oil lamps could have blown out. They had then to be sent to the stores for examination, and if found to be defective, the driver was in trouble, since their maintenance was his responsibility.

Modernisation had been evident earlier on the local trains. By the middle of the 1950s a great many steam stopping services, both on branch and main lines were being displaced by the new diesel railcars, or occasionally by the small 4-wheeled railbuses. By the summer of 1963, steam had disappeared for practical purposes, but the 4.30am from London once again stopped at all stations between Ipswich and Norwich, although Claydon had closed on 17 June 1963 to passengers. The 9.30am all-stations from Ipswich to Norwich still ran, but the end was drawing near for the local trains. The axe fell on Flordon, Forncett, Tivetshall, Burston, Mellis and Finningham on 7 November 1966, when they were closed to passengers; Haughley and Needham survived only

until 2 January 1967. The latter reopened as Needham Market on 6 December 1971, though unstaffed.

The other main line went to King's Lynn, and in some ways its service pattern paralleled that of the Norwich line. An intensive suburban network fed traffic from the branches to Palace Gates, Chingford, Enfield, Buntingford and Hertford East, the latter trains also serving the Lea Valley. Later on the Churchbury loop was reopened and electrified – before the main line, when there was somewhat of a reversal of roles, with the through electric trains to Bishop's Stortford running via the loop and not the main line.

In early British Railways days there was a service to Hertford East at roughly half-hourly intervals, calling at all stations via the Lea Valley, probably excepting Bethnal Green. As with most suburban lines at the time it was enhanced in the morning and evening peaks, with Saturday having its return workings soon after midday, the five and a half day week still being the norm. The first down train in the morning left Liverpool Street at 4.33am, and the last at 11.15pm, the journey taking around 70 min. Connections were provided at Tottenham Hale from Stratford on some trains, and a few started there. The service pattern continued in much the same way throughout the 1950s until the line was electrified in 1960. After that, a half-hourly service ran for most of the day from Liverpool Street to Broxbourne, where trains split for Hertford and Bishop's Stortford; a connecting diesel service called at all stations between Stratford and Cheshunt.

On the other group of inner suburban lines, Chingford enjoyed an all-night service, albeit at infrequent intervals, whilst trains ran at about 10min intervals for most of the day, much enhanced in the peaks when headways could be reduced to 2 or 3min. The Enfield Town service was of the same sort of frequency, and usually all-stations, again much more frequent in the peaks. Both lines had an approximately half-hourly service on Sundays. 'N7s' were the mainstay of these services, and were operated from Stratford and the sub-sheds on the branches.

Palace Gates was served by trains from North Woolwich, and in the early 1950s had a very indifferent service; intensively to the latter in the morning, with the flow going the other way in the

Above:

A Wickham lightweight unit trundles out of Brightlingsea for Wivenhoe where it will connect with a Clacton-Liverpool Street service on 24 July 1960. Following dieselisation in March 1957 passenger traffic increased, but by 1964 the numbers travelling had fallen so much that closure occurred on 15 June.

Frank Church

evenings, most trains from North Woolwich being from 4.7pm to 7.35pm on weekdays. By 1959 the through service was largely unchanged, although between Stratford and North Woolwich there were now roughly two trains an hour. On Sundays, presumably in recognition of the popularity of Alexandra Palace, there was a half-hourly service between Stratford main station (not Low Level) and Palace Gates operated by diesel railcars. The Palace Gates passenger service finished in January 1963.

Turning to the main line, 1951 saw a variety of trains using the Cambridge line from Liverpool Street. King's Lynn was one destination with through services though these were very few; notable was the 'Fenman' to Hunstanton, up from there at 6.45am and back from Liverpool Street at 4.30pm. There were through trains to Norwich, some with a restaurant or buffet car, and they were down at 8.20am, 11.50am, 2.25pm, 5.51pm and 7.20pm. After the introduction of the 'Britannias' these turns would often be covered by them, frequently working out via Ipswich and back via Cambridge, or vice versa. Such trains typically called at Bishop's Stortford, Audley End, Cambridge, Ely and all stations to Norwich, although the 2.25pm was speeded considerably by missing Shippea Hill, Lakenheath, Harling Road, Eccles Road, Spooner Row and Hethersett.

March and Wisbech were other occasional through destinations, the 10.0am train running through from Ely. Cambridge was served off the East Coast main line by the 'buffet expresses' from King's Cross, and was otherwise the most easterly point reached by the former LNWR, who had provided a service from Oxford via Bedford, Bletchley and Bicester. By 1959 there were more through trains to King's Lynn, and the 'Fenman' now carried through coaches for March and Wisbech rather than Bury St Edmunds, the latter having its own restaurant-buffet train at 4.36pm from Liverpool Street. In consequence there were fewer through trains to Norwich, and they no longer carried refreshment facilities.

Of the branches feeding into the line, the service from Thaxted was sparse and did not survive for long, there being five trains on weekdays taking 23min to cover the 5.5 miles of light railway to Elsenham. Saffron Walden did somewhat better, with over 20 trains to or from Audley End in 1951, with 5 extended to Bart-low. The cross-country route from Colchester joined the main line at Shelford, and had a relatively sparse service, there being only five trains each way over its whole length in 1951. Some ran via the Colne Valley route and others via the Stour Valley and Sudbury; others started or finished at intermediate stations, usually Haverhill. Connections were also provided at Long Melford from Bury St Edmunds. It was, however, an important line for cross-country goods and excursion traffic, and saw a number of through trains on summer Saturdays, mainly to Clacton. 'J15s' and 'E4s' were characteristic of the line, although larger locomotives were not unknown, including some of the large 'Austerity' 2-10-0s on occasion.

Cambridge was the focus of other lines, mainly the one from Ipswich via Newmarket, the Mildenhall branch and the St Ives line. The last supported a reasonable service in its own right, and also saw through workings from the London Midland line from Huntingdon East and Kettering. It was also another route to March, this time via the Great Northern & Great Eastern Joint line, which extended thence all the way to Spalding, Sleaford and Doncaster, and which gave the Great Eastern its access to the coalfields. As such it was also an important route to and from the huge marshalling yards at Whitemoor which saw extensive freight traffic to and from London.

Ely, just over 15 miles north of Cambridge, was one of the Great Eastern's most important junctions. Unlike Cambridge no other companies' metals impinged, yet six lines converged on it from King's Lynn, March, St Ives, Cambridge, Newmarket and Thetford. All survive today except the St Ives line, closed to passengers as early as February 1931, but lasting until the Beeching era for freight and excursion traffic. Numbers of through trains to and from the east coast avoided reversal in the station by means

of the curve at Ely North. This permitted through running off the King's Lynn and Norwich lines towards March (and vice versa), which was also important for the sand traffic from Middleton Towers on the Lynn-Dereham line.

King's Lynn was a terminal station, served again by several lines, notably those from Hunstanton, Dereham and Norwich, and South Lynn, where it connected with the M&GN. The Hunstanton line was an interesting and busy one, again receiving considerable holiday traffic. In winter 1955-6 it saw nine trains each way, five either being through services (the 'Fenman') to Liverpool Street, or carrying through carriages. The line was double as far as Wolferton, where an ornate and commodious station had

been built to serve the new royal residence at Sandringham. Heacham had also been a junction (for Wells), but the demise of this line was hastened by flooding in 1952. The line from Dereham saw at least a dozen trains each way on weekdays in the mid-1950s, mostly connecting there to or from Norwich. With the advent of the diesel railcars this changed somewhat, the frequency increasing and some through services now being provided. The last trains ran between Wells and Dereham on 3 October 1965, when the service was run through between Lynn and Norwich, there being nine trains each way, and one extra from each of Dereham and Swaffham. This line lasted for passengers until October 1969.

CHAPTER 11

Great Eastern Goods Services

Norwich was a focus for the local goods traffic, and handled it at Thorpe, Trowse and Victoria. Trains would be despatched to London, being destined principally for the yards at Goodmayes or Spitalfields, or possibly the terminus at Bishopsgate itself. Temple Mills later came to increased prominence with the redevelopment of the marshalling yards there, but tended to handle more of the traffic coming on to the Great Eastern section from other regions such as the Southern or London Midland, or coming in from the docks.

In East Anglia, Lowestoft and Yarmouth were important as fishing ports and despatched several trains per day towards London in the peak of the season; these would usually arrive on the main line via the East Suffolk. This was classed as passenger-rated traffic, and ran as 'Class C' trains, for the obvious reason that fresh fish – even packed in ice – really couldn't be left sweltering in a marshalling yard. Ipswich was a port of considerable importance, and remains so, though now surpassed by Felixstowe. It had an extensive system of dock railways on both sides of the Orwell, some of which is still in use. The rise of Parkeston has been well documented, and although it has been better known in

railway circles for its named boat trains, it has been of the utmost importance in freight terms, and has only recently lost its status as a train ferry terminal. Other smaller ports have also been rail-served, such as Wivenhoe, Brightlingsea and Maldon, all contributing traffic to the main line.

The big yards worked around the clock, and there was much trip working between them, keeping their respective pilots fully occupied. At the same time, there were the smaller depots along the line to be served. In the up direction, the pattern of traffic looked much the same, with a concentration at night. Trains from the country areas would depart in the early evening and arrive in London in the small hours. Many of these trains had been worked as lodging turns – in other words, a Norwich crew might take a goods to Spitalfields one day, run light to Stratford and lodge, and return with a down working the following night. The traffic was extensive in the mid-1950s and a surprising amount was still carried in unbraked wagons which then required working back empty: coal empties gave rise to a huge mileage. Coal, especially for the domestic market, was still in heavy demand and provided a substantial part of the railway's freight revenue.

Other trains, especially the Class K workings which called at every station and siding to pick up or drop traffic, tended to run during daylight hours when station staff were on duty and smaller signalboxes switched in. A working denoted as Class K left Manningtree at 6.25am for Brantham siding, which served the chemical works on the Ipswich side of the station, but the train was officially allowed to propel. It returned at 7.4am. The 6.5am Class K from Ipswich called at Stowmarket, Finningham, Mellis, Diss and Tivetshall, arriving at Trowse at 12.58pm, having shunted each station on the way. Intermediate stations between Ipswich and Stowmarket were covered by the 7.45am, which also called at Bramford siding, serving Messrs Fisons and Pryke Bros. The return working was the 1.40pm Class J all-stations to Ipswich, arriving at 5.38pm.

These Class K trains had been the lifeblood of local communities, even if they had started to be supplanted by the motor lorry in the 1920s and 30s. Everything that was needed in a village arrived or left by train, and the railway had allowed those places it touched to prosper because of the agricultural produce that they could export, or the small works that could be rail-served and so cut the cost of materials and transport of the finished product. One or two illustrations of the sort of activity involved at the smaller stations on the main line in Norfolk and Suffolk are useful. Mellis and Tivetshall were near the top of the league for stations loading grain and flour on the LNER, and considerable tonnages were also on offer at Stowmarket and Needham. Stowmarket and Tivetshall loaded livestock; Needham and Haughley loaded vegetables, though in the latter case much of this was due to the nearby stations of Aspall, Brockford and Mendlesham on the Mid-Suffolk, which came under its jurisdiction. Stowmarket also had traffic in ale and porter, whilst Tivetshall handled round timber. Several stations also had a considerable traffic in manure, and Bramford had enjoyed the dubious distinction of loading more than any other station on the LNER!

Other workings which are worth a mention include some of those which now come under the general heading of 'parcels', which were passenger-rated Class C diagrams. The other example of this type (apart from empty coaching stock) were the fish trains, such as the summer 1957 3.53pm from Lowestoft to Stratford Market, which called only at East Suffolk Junction to change crews, and Witham to let the 4.24pm Sheringham to Liverpool Street express pass. In 1949 there were newspaper trains out of Liverpool Street: the 2.40am for Manningtree, Ipswich and Norwich, due in at 5.37am, was one of the fastest of the day and was converted to 'Britannia' haulage right from their introduction. The same locomotive had worked in with the 9.41pm Class D goods from Thorpe to Spitalfields, due at 2.19am, and which had been a notoriously poor timekeeper until 'Pacifics' were introduced, which cured the problem. The 3.30am 'Newspapers' ran to Chelmsford, Witham, Colchester and Clacton, arriving at 5.44am. The 5.40am empty milk tanks ran from Channelsea Junction to Norwich, calling as required from Haughley to Tivetshall. The 6.59am parcels called at Brentwood, Shenfield and then all stations to Ipswich, and the 12.42pm similarly, replacing

Below left:
The shunter trudges after No D2560 as it potters about the Lower Yard at Ipswich on 5 March 1960. Some of the diesels had skirts fitted for running on the tramways of the quays at Ipswich.
John C. Baker

Below:
'B1' No 61311 runs light through Ipswich station as a Class 31 Brush type 2 diesel approaches with a fitted freight from Parkeston to Whitemoor; 5 March 1960.
John C. Baker

Brentwood and Shenfield with Stratford. The 3.0pm Ocean Mail special ran non-stop to Parkeston, arriving at 4.55pm, and there was an express parcels from Parkeston to Ipswich and March at 7.51pm.

By the 1959-60 timetable, things were looking a great deal thinner in terms of goods workings, even though the wholesale withdrawal of services and the move out of sundries traffic of the Beeching era were still three years away. The effects of line closures were beginning to be seen: the East Suffolk had closed between Beccles and Yarmouth South Town on 2 November 1959, and the Midland & Great Northern in February. Parts of both were retained for local goods, but they were finished as through routes. Traffic was diverted on to the main line as a result: for example, the 12.7am Class D Goodmayes to Lowestoft Central now ran via Wensum Junction as the East Suffolk was closed at night, though the 4.17am Class D Spitalfields to Lowestoft empties (Mondays excepted, as required) did run via Beccles. Temple Mills naturally now played an even more important role in freight workings, and some of the longer distance trains started there, such as the 11.54pm Class E to Goodmayes, Colchester (where it stopped for water only), Ipswich and Trowse. Unbraked

trains such as this continued to be a feature of freight working; trips still included the 1.8am Goodmayes to Colchester, the 9.45am Sproughton to Whitemoor, and the 10.50pm Ipswich to Whitemoor empties, amongst others. Even so, their number was diminishing steadily.

The general pattern of working was still very similar, and showed workings such as the 7.35am Class K Ipswich and all stations to Stowmarket, the trains to Brantham siding from Manningtree, the Hadleigh goods and the leisurely return trip from Trowse to Tivetshall and Bungay. Traffic between Colchester and Cambridge could still run via the Stour Valley, and both Spitalfields and Bishopsgate were still open, though diminishing in the amount of traffic handled, the latter burning down in 1964. It was a particularly rough place, where the men ran the management; when Dr Beeching tried to introduce the 'open terminal' concept whereby traders brought in their goods and loaded and unloaded wagons themselves, there was great opposition from the motor drivers who feared loss of work and employment.

An interesting picture of the pattern of goods traffic was given in the *Eastern Region Magazine* in 1962, which printed maps of England and Wales, showing the density of passenger and freight traffic. As expected, the section between Shenfield and Liverpool Street was the busiest in the country for passengers, though goods traffic in East Anglia showed a different picture. From London to Haughley the main line carried between 10,000 and 50,000 tons per week, whilst the section between Haughley and Norwich managed only between 5,000 and 10,000 tons, with the line to Parkeston similar. Even so, the Beeching report showed Norwich Thorpe, Trowse and Victoria (and City as well) each generating over 25,000 tons per annum, as did Stowmarket, Ipswich, Colchester North and Hythe, Chelmsford and Brentwood. Others fed similar amounts on to the main line, including Yarmouth, Lowestoft Central, Clacton, Felixstowe, Braintree and Maldon, although it didn't stop them being proposed for closure. The only other routes in former Great Eastern territory carrying larger amount of goods traffic were from London to Ely, Haughley to Ely, Norwich to Ely and Cambridge to King's Lynn via March and Wisbech. Norwich then, as now, saw most of its freight going in and out via Thetford; March continued to be the major centre.

Motive power on the Great Eastern lines showed quite a bit of variety over the years. Before the grouping in 1923, the GER had started to provide what were then powerful 4-6-0 locomotives from its works at Stratford; the first of the celebrated '1500' class, then designated 'S69', had been built by Stephen Holden in 1905, and became LNER Class B12. Prior to this, the most powerful express engines had been the 'Clauds' – 4-4-0s to the design of his father James Holden, introduced in 1900. They proved to be very long-lived, some still being in service in 1960 as BR (ex-LNER) Class D16/3, working in most parts of their old parent system – and elsewhere, including the M&GN. Their name was perpetuated on British Railways long after their demise, and the end of steam, in the phrase the 'Claud link': having been displaced many years earlier from front-line duties, they had found employment on the various cross-country and other secondary services in East Anglia. They could be seen operating trains between Norwich and King's Lynn via Dereham, or on the Wells branch. As such they were the province of a peculiarly Great ,Eastern practice, whereby drivers who had been in the top links stepped down on to these less demanding local trains – into the 'Claud link'. They were good-riding, free-steaming engines with 7ft drivers, and were

very sure-footed in dry conditions, though they would slip if given a heavy load on a wet day. By mid-1951 all of the original 'Clauds' had gone, with only 'Super-Clauds' or rebuilds remaining. No 62546 *Claud Hamilton* was condemned in mid-1957, and it is most unfortunate that none of this fine class survived into the preservation era.

The '1500s', later to become the 'B12s', were a significant advance in power and adhesion. They were six-coupled, with 6ft 6in diameter drivers, and were less prone to slipping than the 'Clauds'. They could be fairly heavy on coal, which was improved by Gresley's rebuilding from 1932, when they were given a round-topped firebox in place of the former Belpaire version, and new long-lap valves. For many years they worked on the M&GN on the celebrated 'Leicester', running right through from the east

Below:
The Mildenhall branch was found to have the worst economics of any on the Eastern Region in a 1956 survey. As well as intersecting the main Ipswich-Ely line at Fordham it passed through a number of delightful stations such as Isleham, last one before the terminus.
Lens of Sutton

coast to Birmingham or Leicester until 1956, after which a stop was inserted at Spalding, necessitating reversal and an engine change. Again, many of these engines survived into British Railways ownership, and some indeed, almost to the end of steam. No 61572 is preserved on the North Norfolk Railway at Sheringham.

The next advance on the Great Eastern lines came with the 'Sandringhams' ('B17s' or '2800s'), introduced by H. N. Gresley late in 1928. They offered an increase in power over the '1500s', and had 6ft 8in driving wheels and three cylinders. It could be difficult to detect trouble with the middle big ends, and the solution adopted was to fit a glass container full of aniseed which broke when they ran hot, revealing its presence by smell. They could reach 80mph but had a tendency to roll at speed, especially when eighteen months or so out of the shops and with wear in the axleboxes. In 1935 two of the class were streamlined to work the 'East Anglian', Nos 2859 *East Anglian* and 2870 *City of London*. When introduced on 27 September 1937, the train was allowed 2hr 20min for the journey between Norwich and Liverpool Street, calling only at Ipswich. Although withdrawn for the duration of the war, it was re-introduced in October 1946, but the streamlining was removed from the engines in 1951. Two crews were regularly allocated to each of these engines, which were based at Norwich; 2870 was always considered to be the faster of the two. By

Left:
King's Lynn was another East Anglian terminus, with 'B17' No 61642 *Kilverstone Hall* standing at the platform end having worked in on a 'local' whilst a 'Claud' departs tender-first in the background; September 1957.
Real Photographs K3570

Below:
On the Ely-Ipswich line near Thurston 'K3' No 61942 pilots a 'Britannia' with the Liverpool to Harwich 'North Country Continental' in September 1960. Double-heading of this kind was most unusual on this line.
John C. Baker

1950 members of the class, in common with other express passenger locomotives, had started to appear in the new British Railways dark green livery, and by the start of 1952 all of the class were on the Great Eastern section.

Some of the 'B17s' were rebuilt by Edward Thompson from 1945 as two-cylinder engines, and these were redesignated Class B2. The lack of pits for oiling-up at places such as Colchester gave them an advantage over the inside-cylinder machines, though they were not always liked by the crews. Nevertheless one of the class, No 61671 *Royal Sovereign,* was the official Great Eastern 'Royal Train' locomotive, and at the end of 1950 was still in its LNER apple green livery with bright red bufferbeams and nameplate background.

Further motive power for the Great Eastern main line trains came with Edward Thompson's Class B1 4-6-0s. They were first built in 1942, and in East Anglia at least were known by the name of No 61005 *Bongo,* and many of the class bore the names of species of antelope. They continued to be built by British Railways after nationalisation, and many were allocated from new to Great Eastern sheds, such as Nos 61360/1 in the spring of 1950. No 61057, of Ipswich shed, had to be scrapped after being involved in the Witham accident on 7 March 1950. The 'B1s' had 6ft 2in drivers and were officially mixed traffic engines, though they put up some fine performances on express passenger workings, being able to maintain 'Britannia' timings on occasion. However, thrashing like this caused problems for the boilermakers since it caused the tubes to leak, necessitating their being re-rolled on to the tubeplate.

The 'Britannias' represented the climax of steam power on the Great Eastern. Their introduction en masse was largely due to the vision of Gerard Fiennes, then Assistant Superintendent at Liverpool Street. Together with Stuart Ward he constructed the new regular-interval timetable around their 32,000lb of tractive effort, requiring them to get from Norwich to Liverpool Street in just over two hours, calling only at Ipswich, and to make the return trip twice a day. The first of the class, No 70000 *Britannia* had been officially named at Marylebone station on Tuesday 30 Jan-

uary 1951 by Alfred Barnes, the Minister of Transport, and after spending the afternoon on show, went to Stratford shed via the North London line.

Twenty-three of the new locomotives were allocated to the Great Eastern section from new in 1951, and in spite of teething troubles, settled down to give some sterling performances. They even gave the Great Eastern section Britain's fastest scheduled timings for a brief but glorious period!

Eventually conditions became so bad at Stratford that all the 'Britannia' allocation and maintenance in East Anglia was transferred to Norwich, making a total of 23 engines, although this was down to 16 by the early 1960s. A typical Stratford 'Britannia' turn then involved the North Country boat trains, which might start with a Goodmayes-Ipswich freight; then Ipswich-Parkeston Quay, followed by the boat train to Sheffield. There would be three hours rest there, then back with the night boat train, and back to Spitalfields on a freight. The 'Britannias' averaged about 7,000 miles per month, though No 70012 *Hotspur* did over 10,000 miles in successive months at one time.

After transfer to Immingham they appeared not to be performing as expected, the problem eventually boiling down to the fact that if the engines were to be worked hard and perform well then maintenance had to be very good. For example, they were prone to burn out superheater elements, which thus needed frequent renewal. The piston and valve rings had a low life – seldom over 12,000 miles, and possibly as low as 6,000 miles, whilst the expectation for the BR standards was 36,000 miles; on occasion they had to be renewed every shed day! As with running sheds everywhere, it was sometimes necessary to carry out practical modifications when they arrived from the main shops, making sure to remove them before they returned for overhaul.

Each locomotive was allocated to two drivers; from Norwich, one would take it to Liverpool Street and back in the morning, and the other in the afternoon. Later, a pair of small hooks was fitted on the cab side, and each driver given an engraved nameplate to hang there, so that the public knew who was in charge. As Driver George Ewles once said: 'When a man reached this posi-

tion, he didn't think so much that he worked for the railway, he was so proud he thought he owned it!' The practice was continued in the early days of the new diesels, but didn't persist for long.

Other BR standard locomotives, and some of their LMS predecessors also started to appear in the area. Class 4 2-6-0s were allocated to Melton Constable for the M&GN services, Nos 43147 and 43151 going at the end of 1951, with a further five following at the start of the new year. In mid-1952 Nos 43157-60 were allocated to Yarmouth Beach, followed shortly by No 43161. LMR Class 2s were drafted in to the Colne Valley to replace the 'J15s', Nos 46465-9 being allocated for the purpose, with the first appearing in summer 1951.

There were, of course, many other engines out on the main line apart from the glamorous express locomotives. After the Second World War, the old 'Intermediate' Class E4 2-4-0s could still be seen pottering southward on the main line from Norwich, probably headed for Beccles via Harleston and the Waveney Valley line. They had been introduced in 1891, to the design of James Holden, and had survived to become the last of their wheel arrangement on British Railways; No 490 is presently preserved at Bressingham and is part of the national collection. They could also be seen on the main line taking trains from Colchester to Cambridge via either the Colne or Stour Valley lines, and there was one daily working which required one of these veterans to leave Colchester with eight bogies, tackling the fierce 1 in 123 gradient towards the summit on the London side of Stanway signal box. The train was split at Chappel, both parts going forward to Haverhill by different routes. 'Intermediates' were small and

Facing page, top:
One of the early North British diesels, No D6122, shunts at Thurston with the morning pick-up goods from Ipswich to Bury St Edmunds in January 1960. The motive power may have changed but the shunter's job certainly hasn't.
John C. Baker

Above:
'J17' No 65528 arrives at Bury St Edmunds with a pick-up freight from Sudbury in a scene unchanged in many ways since the engine was built at the turn of the century.
John C Baker

Left:
Bury St Edmunds station seen from the approach road in 1950.
Locomotive & General 27330

light, but usually steamed freely and were extremely simple, as befitted such an old design. The last 'E4', No 62785, survived to haul the last train from Long Melford to Bury before diesel rail-cars arrived on 31 October 1959.

Perhaps the locomotive most typical of the Great Eastern lines in East Anglia was the 0-6-0 Class J15, designed by T. W. Worsdell and first appearing in 1883. Robust and simple engines, they were built in large numbers, eventually totalling 289 by 1913. They had a very low axle loading and hence a route availability of only one, so that they could go almost anywhere, often being the only tender engine permitted over a particular line. They could work ballast trains as far as Tiptree on the Kelvedon & Tollesbury, and they were the only class permitted on the Wisbech Harbour branch. They worked a variety of traffic almost to the last, and although some engines were not fitted with vacuum brakes, they could be seen double-heading excursion trains to the seaside over secondary lines such as the Colne Valley or the Waveney Valley; alternatively, a 'J15' and an 'E4' might provide the power. For example, on 24 August 1952 'J15' No 65471 was piloted by 'E4' No 62789 on a well-filled excursion from Pulham St Mary and Tivetshall Junction to Yarmouth, and it was reported that on the previous Sunday 'J15' No 65469 had worked a similar train unaided. They could even appear on heavy main line trains in emergencies: for example in 1947, when the Cambridge-Ely line was flooded, pairs of them worked expresses over the Barnwell Junction to Fordham section of the Mildenhall branch.

The London area had long been the preserve of various tank engines, and the Great Eastern had been famous for its 'Jazz' service of heavy suburban trains operated with slick precision by seemingly tiny engines. The 'J67-9' series were notable for their feats of haulage, as were the 0-6-2 'N7s', first introduced by A. J. Hill in 1914. There were several variations among their extensive ranks, and they were the backbone of the suburban trains until electrification. Some were replaced by Thompson's 2-6-4 'L1' tanks, and they began to be sent away into the country. One celebrated duty was that of Liverpool Street pilot; in 1957 right-hand drive 'N7' No 69614 was allocated to the west side duty, being turned out in lined black with red coupling rods, all its brass and copper lovingly polished, and even its buffers and smokebox fittings burnished. It covered failures on the 'Jazz' of Hertford or Bishop's Stortford services. Three junior passed firemen were allocated to the east side pilot ('J69' No 68619) which covered the east side shunting and East London trips. George Chittenden, who had just finished on No 70041 *Sir John Moore*, was one of the men on the small pilot, and he and many others spent hours on the paintwork and brightwork in the middle of Liverpool Street station. In fact, if the engine had to go out on the main line there was usually some moaning and groaning!

Other small tank engines still worked many of the branches: 'F5' No 67211 worked the last Braintree to Bishop's Stortford train in March 1952. The last GER 'F3' 2-4-2, No 67127, was withdrawn in May 1953, but the 'F5s' survived to work the Ongar branch until its electrification for London Transport Central Line trains in 1957, and lingered on for working goods until 1959. A few of the similar 'F6s' also survived at Lowestoft and Colchester, occasionally appearing on the Braintree and Maldon branches.

In later days the 'B2s' became very rough, and rode hard; they were so uncomfortable that men would not run fast. The 'B17s' were good engines when well maintained, but did need a hundred per cent, and didn't get it at the end. The 'J39s' were also very heavy on maintenance, and in 1953 a general ban on their working passenger trains was imposed, though the Romford pilot was

a 'J39' and was still used for rescue work in emergencies. However, as late as the start of 1962 No 65567 was on steam heating duties at Norwich Thorpe, being polished up and with gleaming brasswork and red-painted coupling rods. The 'J20s', originally introduced in 1920 by A. J. Hill and subsequently rebuilt with round-topped fireboxes, were good engines, but had small axleboxes and bearings which ran hot easily and so were no use on passenger trains except in an emergency. It was perhaps ironic that the last steam engine into Liverpool Street in September 1962, Class B1 No 61156, was not an original Stratford engine, but a relatively recent arrival.

Diesel locomotives had, of course, begun to supplant steam soon after the war, although it was not until the 1955 Modernisation Plan that they started to appear in any quantity. In 1952 new Drewry diesels, built by the Vulcan Foundry Company, appeared on the Wisbech & Upwell tramway, and Nos 11102/3 were allocated to March for this purpose, with No 11100 going to Ipswich and No 11101 to Yarmouth Vauxhall, both for tramway work. In 1957 the last 'Y4' 0-4-0 No 68126 was replaced at Devonshire Street by diesel shunters Nos 11507/8, although Departmental No 33 (formerly No 68129) was summoned from Stratford to cover for failure on occasion. By the end of 1957 Brush Type 2s including the prototype D5500 – later to become Class 31 – were working some trains out of Liverpool Street, such as the Clactons. They were fitted with 12 cylinder Mirrlees V-form engines developing 1,250hp. On 22 May 1958 D5507 was in charge of the up 'East Anglian' and made the run from Ipswich in 72.25min at a maximum speed of 78mph, whilst on 18 April 1958 D200 had made its historic 'Progress by Great Eastern' demonstration run from Liverpool Street to Norwich, with one stop at Ipswich, covering the 115 miles in 1hr 58.5min. More were allocated to Stratford, with D202-4 arriving in June, together with D5509/10. The 'Britannias' were transferred to Clacton so that those services could be accelerated at the same time. In September an unusual visitor was No 72009 *Clan Stewart* from Carlisle Kingmoor, which was being tried out on the Clacton service. Had it proved to be successful then No 72005-8 would have joined it in exchange for 'Britannias'.

One other locomotive that might have been glimpsed from an Eastern Region train deserves a mention here. The diminutive 0-4-0 geared compound Aveling Porter *Sirapite* had been built in 1906 for the Mountfield Gypsum Mine Tramway and was subsequently sold to Garretts of Leiston. It was used by them for moving wagons in and out of their factory at Leiston, and could be seen in the sidings there. It was quite capable of working the 1 in 37 gradient into their works, and was kept resplendent with its bright green paintwork and polished brass. The curious name arose from the use of gypsum to manufacture plaster of Paris. With the invention of trade names it was not felt appropriate to use 'Parisite', so the 'paris' was duly reversed.

Above right:
This scene has changed dramatically since this was taken in September 1960. LMS '2MT' No 46465 comes off the Wisbech line at March Whitemoor Junction with a General Manager's special. Whitemoor Yard has lost much of its importance, the GN&GE line to Spalding has gone, and the Wisbech line lost its passenger service in 1968.
John C. Baker

Right:
'K3' No 61976 bypasses March station as it comes from Whitemoor with an up freight in September 1960.
John C. Baker

Postscript

In March 1963 Dr Richard Beeching, then Chairman of the British Railways Board, published his report on the reshaping of the railway; most of the country stations on the main lines had closed to all traffic by the end of 1965, leaving only a few to function as 'railheads'. The report observed that the railway system had grown to its full extent when the horse and cart jolting along an unmade road was the only competitor, so rail had penetrated deeply into the local distribution network. Consignment sizes were frequently small and the cost-effective long bulk hauls were few. As roads improved, the advantage of rail disappeared rapidly; for example, 57% of stations open in 1962 contributed only 1% of parcels revenue, and 58% of them generated less than 1% of the minerals and merchandise traffic. Dr Beeching's answer was to concentrate on 'railhead depots' and to develop 'liner trains'. The days of the Class K freight, calling at all stations and ambling along the branches to Eye, Spilsby or Wooler had gone, to be replaced by the block trains of today. When steam finished, the Felixstowe branch contributed almost nothing in freight terms to the main line; now it has the lion's share of the traffic by virtue of the relentless expansion of the port for containers.

Branches would close wholesale, and many of the lines that remained open would lose their local stations, although in the Eastern and North Eastern Regions there were not so many in this category: Lincoln to Grantham, Northallerton to Darlington and from Hartlepool round the coast to Newcastle. Many of the complete closures have been mentioned earlier in the book, together with some that were proposed and stayed open: the East Suffolk, Middlesbrough to Whitby, Darlington to Bishop Auckland. Others seemed to have escaped but later succumbed: the Hunstanton line, Norwich to King's Lynn and the Alnwick branch. A few miles now echo to the sound of preserved trains, and in other places stations and lines have reopened. Unfortunately the financial dice continue to be loaded against the railways and heavily in favour of the roads, and until there is a fundamental reassessment of the position, the successors to Dr Beeching will be forced to continue to cut back. The railways' efficiency has never been higher either in terms of staffing or in energy usage, and after water, they are the most efficient and environmentally-friendly form of transport. Has anything been learned from the Beeching era? We can but await the future with trepidation . . .

Below:
Class D16 4-4-0 No 62567 is seen at Cambridge – a picture which conveys much of the atmosphere of the pre-Beeching railway scene.
Real Photographs/Ian Allan Library